42.00

Teens and PTSD

Peggy J. Parks

ReferencePoint Press®

San Diego, CA

ReferencePoint Press®

For more information, contact:
ReferencePoint Press, Inc.
PO Box 27779
San Diego, CA 92198
www.ReferencePointPress.com

LIBRARY OF CONGRESS CATALOGING-IN-PUBLICATION DATA

Names: Parks, Peggy J., 1951- author.
Title: Teens and PTSD / by Peggy J. Parks.
Description: San Diego, CA : ReferencePoint Press, Inc., 2017. | Series: Teen mental health series | Audience: Grade 9 to 12. | Includes bibliographical references and index.
Identifiers: LCCN 2016042628 (print) | LCCN 2016044253 (ebook) | ISBN 9781682821305 (hardback) | ISBN 9781682821329 (eBook)
Subjects: LCSH: Post-traumatic stress disorder in adolescence--Juvenile literature. | Post-traumatic stress disorder in adolescence--Treatment--Juvenile literature.
Classification: LCC RJ506.P55 P37 2017 (print) | LCC RJ506.P55 (ebook) | DDC 616.85/2100835--dc23
LC record available at https://lccn.loc.gov/2016042628

CONTENTS

A Living Nightmare

Although he was only nine years old at the time, a Maryland teenager named Michael vividly remembers the night his mother was viciously attacked. Michael had been in his bedroom when he heard screaming, and he ran to the kitchen, where he saw his stepfather stabbing his mother repeatedly with a large knife. Only because of Michael's quick thinking did she survive. Trembling with fear, he grabbed a cordless phone, hid beneath an end table, and called 911. "This man is trying to kill my mommy," Michael told the dispatcher, who then heard him scream, "PLEASE! Don't kill her!" When police officers arrived at the house to arrest the man, they found Michael and his two-year-old brother locked in a bedroom. Michael was too terrified to open the door even at the officers' urging. Still talking with the dispatcher, he begged: "May I please wait a few more minutes? Wait. I'm really, really scared."[1]

Traumatized

The boys' mother survived the attack, but the incident left her sons with with emotional scars. Michael was plagued by nightmares in which he relived the violent episode over and over again—hearing the screams, seeing the blood, and feeling the same helplessness and terror. Several years after the incident, he dreamed of hearing a radio news announcer saying on the air that his mother had died. Michael woke up frightened and became frantic when she was not at home. When he finally reached his mother on her cell phone, he was crying hysterically, and she could barely understand what he was saying to her. Through intensive therapy, Michael learned that he suffered from a mental illness called post-traumatic stress disorder, or PTSD, which was a direct result of the trauma he had endured. Psychologist and trauma expert Gretchen Schmelzer defines trauma as an experience or event that overwhelms people's capacities to depend on or protect themselves. "The hallmarks of trauma," says Schmelzer, "are feelings of terror, horror and helplessness."[2]

As with Michael, people develop PTSD after being traumatized in some way, whether it is witnessing an act of brutal violence or living through other types of traumatic events. These include combat duty in a war zone; being a victim of rape, kidnapping, or other violent crime; child sexual or physical abuse; exposure to a terrorist attack; living through a human-made or natural disaster, such as fire, tornado, hurricane, earthquake, or flood; or being in an accident, such as a car wreck in which someone dies or is seriously injured. "It's not unusual for people who have experienced traumatic events to have flashbacks, nightmares, or intrusive memories when something terrible happens," says the Anxiety and Depression Association of America. "Most people who experience such events recover from them, but people with PTSD continue to be severely depressed and anxious for months or even years following the event."[3]

> "The hallmarks of trauma are feelings of terror, horror and helplessness."[2]
>
> —Gretchen Schmelzer, psychologist and trauma expert

Shell Shock

When PTSD was first identified, during the early part of the twentieth century, it was believed to be unique to military personnel who had been deployed in war zones. Initially dubbed "shell shock," it became widely recognized as a serious medical problem among British soldiers who had served in World War I. "The term 'shell shock' was coined by the soldiers themselves," says Edgar Jones, a professor of the history of medicine and psychiatry at King's College London. "Symptoms included fatigue, tremor, confusion, nightmares and impaired sight and hearing. It was often diagnosed when a soldier was unable to function and no obvious cause could be identified." British military officials were blindsided by the onset of the mysterious, often debilitating malady. "Shell shock took the British Army by surprise,"[4] says Jones.

Among soldiers in World War II, the "shell shock" diagnosis was replaced with "combat stress reaction," or as it was commonly known, "battle fatigue." Yet as troublesome and prolific as the disorder was, many people, including top military officials, doubted its validity. The famous World War II general George S. Patton was aghast that seemingly healthy soldiers were too distraught to return to the battlefield. He shouted at them and threatened to court-martial anyone who claimed to have battle fatigue. "Such men are cowards," Patton wrote in an August 1943 memo, "and bring discredit on the Army and disgrace to their comrades

Students visit a memorial following the 2012 school shooting in Newtown, Connecticut. People of all ages can develop PTSD after witnessing or surviving a violent, traumatic event, such as a school shooting.

who they heartlessly leave to endure the danger of a battle which they themselves use the hospital as a means of escaping."[5]

Over the following years perspectives began to change toward the disorder now known as PTSD, with more mental health professionals accepting it as a real illness. After the Vietnam War, which ended in the mid-1970s, researchers took more interest than ever in PTSD because it was such a serious problem among veterans. Tens of thousands returned home suffering from what was then called "post-Vietnam syndrome," prompting the American Psychiatric Association (APA) to recognize "combat trauma" as a psychiatric diagnosis.

In 1980 the APA officially recognized PTSD by including it in the third edition of its *Diagnostic and Statistical Manual of Mental Disorders* (DSM). The manual specified that in order to be diagnosed with PTSD, the patient had to have been exposed to a traumatic event—and for the first time this was not limited to soldiers in combat. Matthew J. Friedman, a psychiatrist and senior adviser to the National Center for PTSD, explains that the APA defined a traumatic event as a "catastrophic stressor that was outside the range of usual human experience." He writes:

> The framers of the original PTSD diagnosis had in mind events such as war, torture, rape, the Nazi Holocaust, the atomic bombings of Hiroshima and Nagasaki, natural disasters (such as earthquakes, hurricanes, and volcano eruptions), and human-made disasters (such as factory explosions, airplane crashes, and automobile accidents). They considered traumatic events to be clearly different from the very painful stressors that constitute the normal [ups and downs] of life such as divorce, failure, rejection, serious illness, financial reverses, and the like.[6]

By including PTSD in its esteemed volume of mental disorders, the APA legitimized a condition that had not always been acknowledged by mental health professionals. Also notable was that in addition to combat-related trauma, the APA included natural disasters, rape, and other traumatic incidents. This was indicative of the association's recognition that PTSD can develop not only in military personnel, but anyone who has been affected by a traumatic experience.

It Can Happen to Anyone

Today, more than thirty-five years after PTSD was formally recognized as a mental health disorder, it remains a topic of extensive scientific study. Researchers have learned a great deal about it, including the various types of trauma that can lead to someone developing PTSD. It is now known that people of all ages can develop PTSD, including teens, after any experience that has traumatized them. This could be anything from witnessing a school shooting to being sexually assaulted or surviving a life-threatening accident.

> "I thought [PTSD] was just for veterans. But I found out it's not; it's for anyone who's experienced an event where you keep thinking about it and it takes over your life."[7]
>
> —Stephanie Romero, a young woman who developed PTSD after being attacked

Stephanie Romero developed PTSD after being the victim of a brutal assault. The night she turned twenty-three, she was out celebrating her birthday with a friend when the two of them were attacked by a stranger. Romero was traumatized by the incident, but she was shocked to learn that she had developed PTSD as a result of it. "I thought it was just for veterans," she says. "But I found out it's not; it's for anyone who's experienced an event where you keep thinking about it and it takes over your life."[7] Although each person with PTSD is different, having the disorder take over their lives seems to be the common thread that binds them together.

CHAPTER ONE

What Is PTSD?

When Kyler Erickson was a senior in high school, he had an experience that was so traumatic it haunted him for a very long time. The incident happened in January 2011 at Millard South High School in Omaha, Nebraska. Erickson had injured his ankle playing basketball the night before and was in the office getting it treated with ice. Suddenly another student, a seventeen-year-old boy who had been suspended that morning, burst through the door and began shooting. Erickson, along with a classmate and two administrators, ran for cover in a bathroom, where they huddled together until they were certain the gunman had left the area. When they slowly opened the bathroom door, they were horrified by the carnage in front of them. The principal and assistant principal had both been shot, and blood covered the people who were trying to assist them. Later at the hospital, the assistant principal died from her injuries. Erickson was devastated by what he had witnessed. He recalls the time he spent hiding, when he could hear what was happening just a few feet away outside the door. "The screams were the worst part," he says. "It was like a horror film but real life. I couldn't get those screams out of my head."[8]

As traumatized as Erickson was by the violent incident, he kept his emotional pain to himself. But his family knew that something was very wrong because of the way his personality changed. He became distant and aloof, no longer his usual happy self. When he left for college, Erickson started to feel as if he was losing his mind. He was plagued by terrifying flashbacks and nightmares, and he began losing his grip on reality. "I was having all these hallucinations . . . all these ghostly figures," he says. "They would have guns and I'd wake up and see them." About a year and a half after the shooting, Erickson realized that he could no longer go on the way he had been, and he opened up to his athletic trainer. Once he was diagnosed with PTSD, he began to understand how profoundly the shooting had affected him. "They kind of think PTSD is just war and people who have returned from war," he says. "It's so much more than that."[9]

Fight or Flight Gone Haywire

As Erickson noted, many people consider PTSD a war-related disorder. Much of what researchers have learned about PTSD was from studying veterans who returned from war zones and were traumatized by the atrocities of combat. But something else researchers have learned in the decades since PTSD was first identified as "shell shock" and "battle fatigue" is that it is not unique to military personnel. Anyone, including teens and young children, can develop PTSD after experiencing something that has traumatized them. "It is a battle most people will never understand," says Stefanie Bagley, who was diagnosed with PTSD when she was fifteen. She says it is a painful disorder, one that is invisible to those who are not affected by it. "You can't SEE who has it and who doesn't," she says. "And by the time you find out who does have it, it may be too late."[10]

To fully understand the complexities of PTSD, it helps to know about a phenomenon called the fight-or-flight response. This is the body's natural, built-in mechanism for reacting to stress or danger. When humans are faced with a threatening situation (or perceive that one exists), fight or flight kicks into gear, triggering a cascade of rapidly occurring reactions. The hypothalamus, a small gland at the base of the brain, prompts the adrenal glands, which sit atop the kidneys, to release a surge of stress hormones, such as cortisol and adrenaline. As these and other hormones course through the bloodstream, the heart rate speeds up and pushes blood into major muscle

> "They kind of think PTSD is just war and people who have returned from war. It's so much more than that."[9]
>
> —Kyler Erickson, a young man who developed PTSD after witnessing a deadly shooting at his high school

PTSD is a painful disorder, and one that is invisible to those who are not affected by it. PTSD symptoms, which can include flashbacks, depression, and nightmares, are severe enough to disrupt a person's life.

groups, which causes muscles to tense. Senses sharpen, digestion slows, energy spikes, and the person becomes more alert and focused. "All of these changes are part of the fight or flight syndrome," says PTSD researcher Matthew Tull. "As the name implies, these changes are preparing you for immediate action. They are preparing you to flee [run away], to freeze (kind of like a deer does when caught in someone's headlights), or to fight."[11]

The fight-or-flight response is essential for human survival. Without it, people would not jump out of the path of a speeding car, take shelter during a tornado, or run from a snarling animal.

A Misunderstood Disorder

When people think about PTSD, they typically associate it with members of the military who have experienced trauma in combat. But according to a 2016 Drexel University study, more civilians suffer from PTSD than do military personnel—thirteen times more. Another common misperception about PTSD is that symptoms appear immediately after traumas occur, but it can take months or even years after a traumatic experience for symptoms to appear. Also, some people mistakenly believe that people with PTSD will exhibit violent behavior. Yet the majority of those with the disorder have never experienced a violent episode.

Another mistaken belief about PTSD is that it can be inherited. But, as the name suggests, it takes a traumatic event to trigger PTSD in an individual. Although PTSD itself is not passed through genes, people with some traits, such as anxiety and depression, which do have a genetic component, are at higher risk for developing PTSD. However, they still must experience a traumatic event in order to develop the disorder.

Friends and family members of people with PTSD may believe that the symptoms the individuals exhibit are imagined, that PTSD is not a real disorder, or that the individuals are behaving that way only to get sympathy and attention. But PTSD is classified as a mental disorder by the APA, and the symptoms displayed by those with PTSD are a very real reaction to an extremely disturbing and traumatic event.

"The human race may not even exist if it were not for these hardwired responses to danger and threat," says Tull. "Anxiety and fear provides us with information. That is, they tell us when danger is present and they prepare us to act."[12]

For most people, once the danger has passed or the perceived threat no longer exists, the body returns to its natural state. Hormones level out, and the heart rate slows. Muscles relax, and other systems normalize. But the same is not true for those with PTSD, whose fight-or-flight responses do not switch off like they should. Rather, their brains stay locked in high-alert mode, as though danger was imminent. "When people experience something traumatic and/or have PTSD," says Tull, "they may no longer feel as though the world is a safe place. It may feel as though danger is everywhere. As a result, a person may constantly be in a state of fear and anxiety."[13]

Cat P., a twenty-one-year-old woman who writes online about her difficulties coping with PTSD, describes it as "being in constant fight-or-flight mode." Cat has experienced multiple traumas throughout her young life and says she spends much of her time afraid, even when her rational mind knows there is nothing to fear. "Right now I am scared," she says. "My body is in fight-or-flight mode, just as it would be if I were running from a bear chasing after me, but there is no real danger." Cat is well aware of how other people likely perceive her. "To others, I can seem attention-seeking, melodramatic and even 'crazy' at times," she says. "All I can say to that is, I can assure you this is as real to me as is the air you breathe. If I had control over it, then I would not be experiencing it."[14]

Beyond Anxiety

As more has been learned about PTSD, mental health experts have changed how it is classified in terms of diagnosis. Prior to 2013, for instance, PTSD was considered one of the anxiety disorders, a group of mental illnesses that are characterized by extreme fear, worry, and distress. That changed with the APA's fifth version of the DSM (DSM-5). Although PTSD shares many similarities with anxiety disorders, it is now included in a new category called Trauma- and Stressor-Related Disorders. Sara Staggs, a senior trauma therapist at the DC Rape Crisis Center in Washington, DC, says placing PTSD in the new category could help destigmatize the disorder "since it is no longer an anxiety related mental illness, but a disorder connected to an external event,"[15] meaning some kind of traumatic experience.

> "When people experience something traumatic and/or have PTSD, they may no longer feel as though the world is a safe place. It may feel as though danger is everywhere."[13]
>
> —Matthew Tull, a researcher who specializes in PTSD

According to the APA, this trauma could include a close brush with death or being threatened with death, as well as some kind of exposure to serious injury or sexual violence. "The victim may experience the event, witness it, learn about it from close family members or friends, or experience repeated or extreme exposure to aversive details of the event," says psychiatrist Roy H. Lubit. "Potentially traumatic events include physical or sexual assaults, natural disasters, and accidents."[16]

Flashbacks and Nightmares

In order to be diagnosed with PTSD, a person must have had symptoms lasting for one month or longer that are severe enough to interfere with the person's life. Teens, for instance, may suddenly have trouble sleeping, lose interest in favorite activities, and/or see a significant drop in their grades. They may also start having physical problems, such as stomachaches and/or headaches.

The APA divides PTSD symptoms into four distinct clusters: reexperiencing, avoidance, negative changes in beliefs and feelings, and arousal. Reexperiencing brings the traumatic experience back to life over and over again. This often involves nightmares, as well as flashbacks, which may be images, sounds, smells, or a combination of them. Flashbacks are not just memories of the trauma—they are sudden, vivid reminders of it that are so intense and realistic the person feels like he or she has been transported back in time and is reliving it. Stanford Children's Health writes: "Children and adolescents with PTSD experience extreme emotional, mental, and physical distress when exposed to situations that remind them of the traumatic event. Some may repeatedly relive the trauma in the form of nightmares and disturbing recollections during the day."[17]

"Children and adolescents with PTSD experience extreme emotional, mental, and physical distress when exposed to situations that remind them of the traumatic event."[17]

—Stanford Children's Health, a renowned children's hospital located in Palo Alto, California

Prevalence of Trauma Puts Youth at Risk of PTSD

Young people who experience traumatic events such as assault, physical abuse, rape, or violence at home or in their community are at risk of developing PTSD. According to a 2016 report from the nonprofit research organization Child Trends, a surprisingly high percentage of young people have been exposed to violence of this sort. This exposure increases the likelihood of PTSD developing in some of these young people.

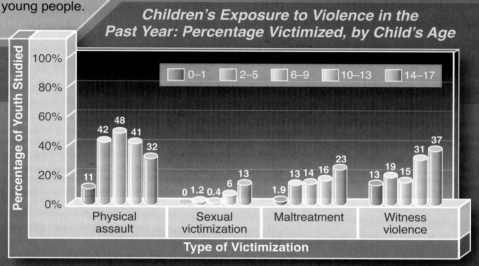

Children's Exposure to Violence in the Past Year: Percentage Victimized, by Child's Age

Source: Child Trends Databank, "Children's Exposure to Violence," May 2016. www.childtrends.org.

Soon after Kyler Erickson left for college, he started having flashbacks of the deadly shooting at his high school. When he was in his dormitory room, sudden bangs or loud noises from other rooms or hallways were unbearable reminders of the horrors he had witnessed, and sometimes he sobbed uncontrollably. "I curled up in this ball and was just covering my ears," he says, "and people would ask me, 'What are you doing?'"[18]

Nightmares can be just as traumatic as flashbacks for PTSD sufferers. California psychiatrist Shaili Jain describes nightmares as "those threatening or scary dreams that leave you crying out in your sleep, thrashing around in your bed or waking up in a blind panic, soaked in sweat and with your heart pounding in your throat." According to Jain, who specializes in PTSD, nightmares are "a very common complaint for those living with PTSD."[19]

Recognizing Her Own PTSD

Sarah Newman, a young woman who was sexually abused as a child, had trouble making the connection between that abuse and the anxiety she had felt all her life. She also did not recognize that she was suffering from PTSD. It did not seem possible that her childhood trauma could lead to the same disorder as that experienced by combat veterans. Newman writes:

> I lived in denial of the sexual abuse I experienced as a child. I saw therapists throughout my life and was treated for anxiety and depression. Because I didn't recognize what happened to me as sexual abuse—I was too young when it occurred to understand what was happening— I never brought it up in therapy. It was a blind spot in my personal narrative.
>
> I never considered that my anxiety and hypervigilance could be related to PTSD. I felt that the absence of flashbacks meant it couldn't be relevant. . . .
>
> Even after the fog of denial lifted and I started talking about the abuse in therapy, I still had trouble seeing myself as someone with PTSD. I began comparing my trauma to the trauma of others. I was imagining some hierarchy where I didn't have a right to be so traumatized. I mean, what could be more traumatic than seeing someone die? Those people need more help than me, right? That kind of thinking wasn't helpful.

Sarah Newman, "How Media Shapes Our View of Post-Traumatic Stress Disorder," *World of Psychology* (blog), Psych Central, June 10, 2016. http://psychcentral.com.

She says that people continue to be haunted by nightmares for months or even years after the traumatic event took place. For teen PTSD sufferers who are already going through stressful life changes, recurring nightmares can be debilitating.

Sally, a teenage girl from Vermont, started having terrifying nightmares as a result of a traumatic, life-threatening experience that took place when she was fourteen. It was a cold winter day, and Sally was riding in a car driven by her brother. Suddenly he hit a patch of black ice and spun out of control, which caused the car to flip over onto its side and then come to rest upside down on its roof. Sally's brother suffered a fractured skull but survived the horrific crash. Sally was trapped for an hour under the compressed windshield until rescuers could get to her. According to adolescent psychiatrist Steven Schlozman, Sally's nightmares started the second night after the crash. "In her dream," says Schlozman, "the car would spin in slow motion, and she would wake with the very vivid image of her brother (who she was certain was dead at the time of the actual accident) as if he were in her bedroom."[20] Sally's parents were able to calm her down that night, but the nightmares continued and grew worse, until she was afraid to sleep at all.

Other PTSD Characteristics

Along with nightmares and flashbacks, which are classic PTSD re-experiencing symptoms, avoidance symptoms are also common among PTSD sufferers. True to its name, the avoidance category includes behavioral tactics that PSTD sufferers use in an effort to avoid being exposed to anything that reminds them of the traumatic event. This may involve staying away from people, places, or activities that trigger memories of the experience. "For people with PTSD, it is very common for their memories to be triggered by sights, sounds, smells or even feelings that they experience," says psychologist David Riggs, an expert on trauma and PTSD. "These triggers can bring back memories of the trauma and cause intense emotional and physical reactions, such as raised heart rate, sweating and muscle tension." Because these memories and feelings are unpleasant, says Riggs, for PTSD sufferers to avoid anything that triggers them is a normal reaction. "But in the long run," he says, "this avoidance will make things worse."[21]

The third group of PTSD symptoms includes negative changes in beliefs and feelings. "The way you think about yourself and others may change because of the trauma,"[22] says the National Center for PTSD. The person may experience a wide range of emotions, from overpowering guilt, worry, or depression to feeling emotionally numb. Also common is for PTSD sufferers to lose interest in activities they used to enjoy and to perceive their surroundings as dangerous, with no one they can trust.

Arousal (sometimes called hyperarousal) is the fourth cluster of PTSD symptoms, and it essentially means feeling keyed up and jittery. People with PTSD may constantly feel tense and on edge, are easily startled, and are always alert for potential threats or danger. They may find it difficult to concentrate and have trouble sleeping at night because their anxiousness keeps them from being able to relax.

Troubled Teens

The Brain & Behavior Research Foundation states that teens with PTSD usually show symptoms that are consistent with those of adults, although young people may also develop "disruptive, disrespectful or destructive behaviors."[23] Older children and teens, the group adds, sometimes feel crushing guilt for not being able to prevent injury or deaths that may have occurred. Additional symptoms that are common among teens with PTSD include problems sleeping, weight gain or weight loss, and an overall sense of frustration and melancholy.

After Eyama Harris went through a traumatic, life-changing experience, she did not recognize the danger signs and had no idea that she had developed PTSD. Harris was fifteen years old when her mother was murdered, and the teen was devastated. "I tried everything I could to deal with my feelings, including writing songs," she says. "But still, something was different about me. I noticed that I didn't feel like my normal self anymore, not only mentally, but physically. I was losing weight, and my hair was falling out."[24] According to the doctor who first saw Harris, her symptoms were a clear warning that things were not going well for her. Once she was diagnosed with PTSD, she could finally begin healing from the trauma that had haunted her.

According to Elements Behavioral Health, one important difference between teens and adults with PTSD is that teens have a tendency to experience something called post-traumatic reenactment. "During post-traumatic reenactment," the group writes, "an affected individual will start engaging in behaviors that mimic some feature of a traumatic event. For instance, a teenager exposed to gunfire might suddenly start carrying a gun."[25] In addition, teens are more likely than adults to exhibit impulsive and aggressive behaviors as a result of PTSD.

PTSD Prevalence

Not everyone who has experienced trauma develops PTSD. In fact, most do not. Schlozman explains: "While almost 90% of individuals will have symptoms of PTSD after a trauma, these symptoms abate in almost everyone after roughly a month's time—this is called an *acute stress disorder*."[26] According to Schlozman, of those who have experienced trauma, about 30 percent develop PTSD.

Far fewer teens have PTSD than adults—but studies show that an alarming number of youth are exposed to violence and are therefore at high risk for PTSD. According to a 2016 report by the research organization Child Trends, 32 percent of teens were physically assaulted during 2014; 13 percent were sexually victimized in some way (such as date rape or attempted rape); 23 percent suffered some kind of maltreatment; and 37 percent witnessed violence in the home and/or community. The report authors write: "An experience of violence can lead to lasting physical, mental, and emotional harm, whether the child is a direct victim or a witness."[27] Although the authors do not specifically cite PTSD as a result of the teens' trauma, it is widely known that risk for the disorder is markedly higher among teens who are abused or exposed to physical or sexual violence than among other teens.

Research has shown that an estimated 5 percent of teenagers in the United States meet the criteria for PTSD. The risk is significantly higher for teenage girls, whose likelihood of developing the disorder is more than three times higher than that of boys. According to the National Center for PTSD, there are several reasons for this discrepancy. Girls are more likely to experience sexual assault, sexual assault is more likely to cause PTSD than many other traumatic incidents, and girls are more likely than boys to blame themselves for trauma experiences. In general, the risks for both teenage girls and boys rise as they get older.

Children of War

Most people are aware of the high prevalence of PTSD among military personnel, especially those who are serving or have served in combat zones. But research has also shown that civilians in war-torn regions of the world, where they spend day after day in an environment of hostility and violence, have a high risk of PTSD. This is especially true of young people, who develop PTSD as often, or even more often, than soldiers in combat.

Numerous studies have focused on teens who live in Gaza, a small Palestinian territory on the eastern coast of the Mediterranean Sea that is bordered by Israel and Egypt. For many years, due to irreconcilable conflicts between the Palestinians and Is-

A man carries a young girl away from a bombed-out building in Aleppo, Syria, in 2016. Research has shown that children who live in war-torn regions of the world have a high risk of PTSD, developing it as often as soldiers in combat.

raelis, Gaza has been ravaged by war. This has created a violent, dangerous environment for young people, and as a result, an extraordinary number of them suffer from PTSD. One 2014 study involved 358 Palestinian teens aged fifteen to eighteen who live in Gaza. The researchers found that 92 percent of the teens had PTSD symptoms, and 30 percent had full-blown PTSD—at least six times the number of teens affected by PTSD in the United States. An earlier study was even more disturbing. It found that nearly 33 percent of Gazan youth between the ages of ten and nineteen exhibited signs of severe PTSD, while almost half showed signs of moderate PTSD.

A particularly shocking finding of the most recent study of Gazan teens was how much violence they had seen firsthand. Most reported that they had viewed mutilated bodies on television, had been in close proximity to heavy artillery shelling, had heard the deafening sounds of fighter jets overhead, had witnessed people being killed by rockets, or had learned that a friend or relative had been killed. The study authors write: "The present study highlighted the intensity and severity of traumatic events during the war and the lasting effect of adolescent tendencies to store memories of the traumatic events for much longer than expected." The authors add that "there was strong association between total traumatic events and PTSD."[28]

Hard to Cope

PTSD develops as a direct result of being traumatized. People of all ages can suffer from the disorder, including children and teens, and it causes a number of difficult, sometimes terrifying, symptoms: experiencing vivid flashbacks, horrific nightmares, and inexplicable fears; seeing and hearing things that are not really there; and feeling keyed up and jittery. PTSD is not a visible disorder; people do not always know when someone has it, and they often do not understand what it is anyway. But for those who suffer from PTSD, life can sometimes feel unbearable.

CHAPTER TWO

What Causes PTSD?

Many physical diseases have clearly defined causes, such as bacteria or viruses. But the same cannot be said of mental illness, whose causes are much more difficult to pinpoint. PTSD, for instance, is always rooted in some kind of trauma, but other factors are involved in its development as well. If trauma alone were the cause of PTSD, every person who has been traumatized would have the disorder, and that is not the case. "More than 60 percent of teenagers have experienced a traumatic event in their lifetime," says Boston Children's Hospital researcher Daniel Busso, "but only a minority will develop post-traumatic stress disorder (PTSD). For both researchers and clinicians, this raises an important question: Why are some youth at greater risk for mental health problems after trauma?"[29] Although research revelations have helped scientists better understand PTSD, there is still much about its development that remains unknown.

Complexities Abound

According to the National Center for PTSD, 15 percent to 43 percent of girls have at least one traumatic experience, and 3 percent to 15 percent of them go on to develop PTSD. Among boys, 14 percent to 43 percent experience trauma at least once, and of those, 1 percent to 6 percent develop PTSD. These numbers strongly suggest that trauma alone does not cause PTSD.

Studies with PTSD patients have revealed that the development of the disorder depends on people's individual capacity to cope with trauma; some people are more vulnerable to the effects of trauma than others. "While most people exposed to traumatic events do not develop PTSD," says psychiatrist Matthew J. Friedman, "others go on to develop the full-blown syndrome." Friedman theorizes that people have different "trauma thresholds," with some "more protected from and some more vulnerable to developing clinical symptoms after exposure to extremely stressful situations."[30]

In a September 2015 paper, psychologist Gretchen Schmelzer also discusses trauma and people's individual ability to cope with it—which varies from person to person. "Trauma affects everyone differently," she says. "There's no 'one-size-fits-all' response because trauma affects you differently based on how you were before it hit: what level of stress you were under, your health, your stage of development, previous experience of trauma and the resources you have available to you." When parents ask Schmelzer how long it will take their teens to recover from a traumatic experience, she uses the metaphor of a car accident to help explain:

> If you were in a car accident—there would be no "simple" answer to, "How long will it take to recover?" It would depend on how bad the accident was and how you were doing before the accident. If you were perfectly healthy and the accident wasn't too bad, the recovery might be relatively quick. If you had just gotten out of the hospital from surgery, or had a previous traumatic brain injury then recovery could be months, or even years. Trauma is like a car accident for the emotional being.[31]

Researchers have identified a number of factors that can increase someone's chances of developing PTSD after he or she has endured a traumatic experience. One factor is genetics, since the disorder runs in families. This has been revealed in studies with twins, which have shown that identical twins are much more likely to both develop PTSD compared with fraternal twins. "Individuals may have genetic or other biological predispositions to developing post-traumatic stress disorder," says adolescent psychiatrist Steven Schlozman. He clarifies, however, that this happens in conjunction with trauma. "The cause of post-traumatic symptoms is always an external event."[32]

Known Risk Factors

Along with an individual's family history, other factors can play a role in PTSD's development, such as the severity of the trauma. Research has established that severe traumatic events (such as rape or other violent personal crimes) are most often associated with PTSD. Also relevant in teens developing PTSD is how parents react to the child's experience with trauma. "PTSD symptoms may be less severe if the child has more family support and if the parents are less upset by the trauma," says the National Center for PTSD. The teen's proximity to the source of trauma (such as a violent crime or terrorist attack) can also help determine whether he or she develops PTSD, as the group explains: "Children and teens who are farther away from the event report less distress."[33] In addition, teens who have endured multiple traumas have a higher risk of developing PTSD.

> "The cause of post-traumatic symptoms is always an external event."[32]
>
> —Adolescent psychiatrist Steven Schlozman

A large 2013 study by researchers from Boston Children's Hospital sought to identify teens who were especially vulnerable to developing PTSD. The researchers, led by clinical psychologist Katie McLaughlin, analyzed data on 6,483 teens aged thirteen to seventeen and their parents from a national survey. The analysis found that more than 61 percent of the teens had been exposed to at least one potentially traumatic event in their lifetime. These included interpersonal violence (such as rape, physical abuse, or witnessing domestic violence); physical injuries; natural disasters; and death of a close friend or family member. The study also found that 19 percent of the teens had experienced three or more traumatic events. Of those who were exposed to trauma, 4.7 percent had gone on to develop PTSD.

The top two risk factors that were strongly associated with the teens' exposure to trauma included the absence of two biological

Factors That Increase Risk

An important aspect of PTSD is that all those who develop it have endured some type of traumatic event. Although most teens who experience trauma suffer some level of emotional distress, the majority do not develop PTSD. Shown here are risk factors that increase the likelihood of a teenager developing the illness.

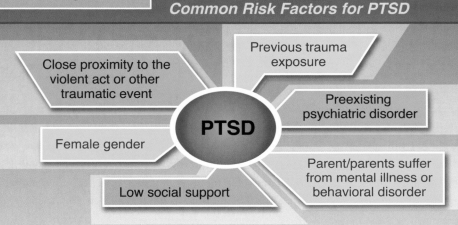

Common Risk Factors for PTSD

- Previous trauma exposure
- Close proximity to the violent act or other traumatic event
- Preexisting psychiatric disorder
- Female gender
- Parent/parents suffer from mental illness or behavioral disorder
- Low social support

PTSD

Source: National Center for PTSD, "PTSD in Children and Adolescents," Jessica Hamblen and Erin Barnett, February 23, 2016. www.ptsd.va.gov.

parents in the home, and preexisting mental disorders, especially attention-deficit/hyperactivity disorder and oppositional defiant disorder, in which a child or teen exhibits frequent, persistent anger, irritability, arguing, and defiance. Risk factors identified by the researchers included the following:

- Female gender: Girls were shown to have a lifetime prevalence of PTSD of 7.3 percent, compared with 2.2 percent for boys.
- Events involving interpersonal violence: The lifetime prevalence of PTSD was 39 percent for teens who had been raped and 25 percent for teens who were physically abused by a caregiver.
- Accompanying mental health issues: Anxiety and mood disorders were found to increase teens' likelihood of developing PTSD.

Big-T and Little-T Traumas

There are different levels of trauma that can lead to PTSD. People can develop the disorder as the result of experiencing what are known as "Big-T" or "little-t" traumas. Big-T traumas include catastrophic or life-threatening events, such as a natural disaster, a serious car accident, combat, and physical or sexual assault. Such traumas have a significant impact on the brains of individuals who experience them, but it is not only the Big-T events that can lead to PTSD. Mental health experts have learned that smaller, little-t traumas can have the same neurological impact as Big-T traumas.

Little-t traumas include experiences such as being bullied, the death of a family member or pet, a minor car accident, parents divorcing, or a relationship breakup. Although not life-threatening, little-t events are still frightening, unsettling, and traumatic or upsetting to those who experience them. And even though they are less intense, little-t traumas can impact a person's emotional and social development just as much as the bigger, more catastrophic Big-T traumas. Big-T traumas are more serious in nature and produce more intense symptoms of PTSD, but they are also less common. Far more common are the little-t traumas, which can lead to less severe PTSD symptoms, such as worrying, sadness, or avoidance of situations that are similar to the ones that led to the trauma.

In an editorial that accompanied the study, Julian D. Ford, a professor of psychiatry in the School of Medicine at the University of Connecticut, writes: "Ultimately, this study is a poignant reminder that millions of adolescents in this country are growing up under the long shadow cast by exposure to traumatic stressors."[34]

Clues Within the Brain

When researchers study the effects of trauma on teens, a major focus is on the brain; specifically, how certain regions of the brain respond to trauma and how that might influence whether someone develops PTSD. As Busso explains: "Studies suggest that disruptions to the body's stress response system, or in patterns of brain activity when responding to threat, may predispose people to the disorder."[35]

One study that examined the effects of trauma on the adolescent brain was conducted by researchers from Boston Children's Hospital, Harvard Medical School, Boston University, and the University of Washington. A group of forty teens from the Boston, Massachusetts, area underwent magnetic resonance imaging (MRI) brain scans to evaluate their responses to emotional stimuli. For instance, the teens viewed a series of negative images (showing people who were sad, fighting, or threatening someone) and neutral images (such as a chair or button). As the teens reviewed the negative and neutral images, MRIs measured blood flow to the amygdala region of the brain, which plays a primary role in processing emotions such as fear, anger, and pleasure; and the hippocampus, which is involved with forming, storing, and processing memory.

The second phase of the study was unplanned—and came about as the result of a national tragedy. On April 15, 2013, terrorists exploded two bombs near the finish line of the Boston Marathon, killing 3 spectators (including an eight-year-old boy) and injuring more than 260 others. Members of the collaborative research team wanted to know whether the teens who had participated in their study had experienced any PTSD symptoms as a result of the terrorist attack. They contacted the teens who had been in Boston on April 15, and fifteen of them agreed to be part of the second phase of the study. The teens filled out online surveys with questions such as whether they had been near the finish line during the bombing, how much media coverage they were exposed to after the attack, whether they were part of the lockdown at home or school while law enforcement hunted for the suspects, and how their parents reacted to the incident. The researchers also asked about specific PTSD symptoms, such as whether the teens had trouble concentrating and whether they kept thinking about the bombing even when they tried not to.

By using MRI scans from before the attack combined with survey data after the attack, the researchers made a profound discovery. They found a significant connection between heightened activity in the teens' amygdalas and the development of PTSD later. According to Busso, this shows that "activity in the amygdala in response to distressing images did indeed predict the severity of PTSD symptoms after the bombings."[36] Busso says other factors were identified that also predicted increased risk for PTSD among teens. These included a prior experience of violence, such as getting mugged or witnessing someone else getting mugged, and prior histories of anxiety and depression.

Traumatized by Sexual Abuse

Of all the ways that young people are abused, sexual abuse is one of the most traumatic. It is also among the top contributors to the development of PTSD. "Sexual abuse is a particularly sinister type of trauma because of the shame it instills in the victim," says Susanne Babbel, a psychologist who specializes in trauma. "With childhood sexual abuse, victims are often too young to know how to express what is happening and seek out help. When not properly treated, this can result in a lifetime of PTSD, depression and anxiety." According to the US Department of Justice, an estimated one in six boys and one in four girls in the United States are sexually abused before age eighteen, and this abuse is most often by someone the children know. "Some of the most startling statistics unearthed during research into sexual abuse are that children are three times as likely to be victims of rape than adults," says Babbel, "and stranger abuse constitutes by far the minority of cases. It is more likely for a child to experience sexual abuse at the hands of a family member or another supposedly trustworthy adult."[37]

> "Sexual abuse is a particularly sinister type of trauma because of the shame it instills in the victim."[37]
>
> —Susanne Babbel, a psychologist who specializes in trauma

A 2013 paper by researchers from Quebec, Canada, discusses how closely connected child sexual abuse is with PTSD. "Overall," the authors write, "victims have been shown to present significantly more [PTSD] symptoms than non-abused children, or than victims of other forms of trauma."[38] They go on to describe one of their studies in which the mental health of sixty-

Sexual abuse is among the top contributors to the development of PTSD, and one in four girls in the United States is sexually abused before the age of eighteen.

seven sexually abused school-aged girls was compared with the same number of girls (the control group) who had not been victims of sexual abuse. The girls with a history of child sexual abuse were found to develop PTSD at a rate that was four times higher than the girls in the control group. The researchers write: "These results have echoed previous research conducted among . . . sexually abused school-aged children and teenagers where about a third to a half of all victims showed clinical levels of post-traumatic stress symptoms."[39]

One teenage girl who developed PTSD after being raped was fifteen-year-old Maria. One day as she walked home from school, she was brutally attacked by a group of men. They screamed

Violent News and PTSD in Teens

One theory about PTSD in teens is that it can result from viewing violent news stories. Newspaper articles, TV news programs, and social media newsfeeds are filled with accounts of subway bombings, mass shootings, and terrorists executing civilians. It is normal for people to want to keep informed of events that take place around the world, but according to experts, too much exposure to violence can lead to symptoms of PTSD in teens. The frequency and amount of violence teens view on social media and in the news can increase their levels of anxiety and fear, even though they are not in any actual danger themselves. Psychologist Anita Gadhia-Smith says, "With the frequency of shooting and terror attacks there is a sense of anxiety that's building in people, a sense of vulnerability and powerlessness."

The connection between viewing violent news stories and developing PTSD-like symptoms was examined in a 2015 study conducted by a team of researchers at the University of Bradford in England. In the study, 189 participants were exposed to images and stories of violent events such as school shootings and suicide bombings. The researchers found that 22 percent of the participants were deeply disturbed by the violent images and stories. In addition, the researchers found that people who viewed violent news more frequently suffered from more of a negative impact than people who viewed violent news less frequently.

Quoted in Katie Rogers, "What Is a Constant Cycle of Violent News Doing to Us?," *New York Times*, July 15, 2016. www.nytimes.com.

abusive words at her as they raped her one by one. Then they attempted to stab her to death, but their efforts were thwarted, as Harold Cohen writes on Psych Central: "[They] would almost certainly have succeeded had the police not arrived on the scene."[40]

Soon after the attack and for months afterward, Maria was haunted by flashbacks of the horrific attack. At night she was plagued by nightmares of the rape and often woke up screaming. She could not stand walking home from school her usual way because it took her past the site of the attack, so she had to walk home the long way. "She felt as though her emotions were numbed," says Cohen, "and as though she had no real future. At home she was anxious, tense, and easily startled. She felt 'dirty' and somehow shamed by the event, and she resolved not to tell close friends . . . in case they too rejected her."[41] Only after Maria confided in a teacher she trusted did she start feeling as if maybe there was hope for her after all.

The Trauma of Serious Accidents

Although many people know about the relationship between sexual assault and PTSD, they may not know that it can also follow serious motor vehicle crashes. According to the Centers for Disease Control and Prevention (CDC), teenage drivers are involved in fatal motor vehicle crashes nearly 200 percent more often than drivers who are age twenty or older. Also, motor vehicle crashes are the leading cause of death for teens in the United States. Young people who survive these crashes may be traumatized in several ways, such as being seriously injured and requiring hospitalization; witnessing serious injuries of others involved in the crash or seeing them dead; and experiencing what is known as survivor's guilt, which is wishing they had done or said something that might have prevented the crash from happening.

Witnessing a serious injury in a car crash traumatized a teenage boy named Eric. He was riding to the mall with his mother when a car ran a red light and hit the side of her car, causing it to spin out and slam into a tree. Eric and his mom were not hurt, but the driver who hit them sustained a serious head injury. Although relieved that he and his mom were okay, Eric was extremely upset to see blood coming from the man's wound and trickling down his forehead onto his face.

After the crash Eric became terrified of being in cars. Even walking down the street scared him because, as he said, there were "crazy drivers everywhere" and he was worried about being hit. He had nightmares about car crashes and was haunted by the memory of the man's head wound, saying it was "like a color picture in my head."[42] Eric's personality changed too. Formerly outgoing and active, he became reclusive, staying at home and arguing with his mom about going to school. He became anxious whenever he heard a car horn honking, and he refused to watch any television shows that contained violence. The crash had affected Eric deeply and led to his development of PTSD.

Kids Caught in the Crossfire

Another cause of PTSD in young people is where they live; specifically, those who live in inner cities where violent crime is rampant. According to the CDC, up to 30 percent of teens living in these crime-ridden areas have PTSD, compared with the national average of 5 percent. Many experts say that inner-city youth have a higher prevalence of PTSD than soldiers—but unlike soldiers, who eventually leave combat zones, young people in inner cities are trapped in the midst of the violence, which can lead to severe trauma and ultimately PTSD. "A soldier goes to war and they come home and they've left the battlefield," says Anne Marks, executive director of the Oakland, California, violence prevention and youth leadership organization Youth Alive! "We work with young people who get shot, go to the hospital, get their treatment, and go back to the same community, maybe the same home they were shot in front of. Maybe there are bullet holes in the door. So there's no 'post' in the traumatic stress. It's continuing traumatic stress disorder."[43]

One area where violent crime is a constant problem, especially gang-related gun violence, is South Los Angeles, California. Children and teens have been injured or killed while walking to school, riding skateboards, riding in a car, or even just standing on a front porch talking with their friends. In September 2015 an eleven-year-old boy and thirteen-year-old girl were shot while waiting to be served at a South Los Angeles taco stand. A few months prior to that, a teenage boy was shot and killed at a car wash for refusing to give up his red shoes. In July 2015 a teenage boy was shot multiple times while riding his bicycle, and he died at the hospital. In this dangerous environment, where violence and fear are inextricably woven into young people's day-to-day living, the incidence of PTSD is soaring.

Courtney Pender, a psychiatric social worker at Washington Prep High School in South Los Angeles, sees the struggles, losses, and grief these young people must endure day after day.

They suffer from PTSD while having to live in an environment of rampant violence. "We have a number of students that are struggling with issues associated with traumatic loss or traumatic experiences associated with community violence,"[44] says Pender. During a screening program at the school, 55 percent of the students tested were found to be within clinical range of PTSD. Many do not care whether they go to school at all—which according to Pender is understandable. "If you're trying to take a test and you're starting to have flashbacks of seeing your mom in a casket, then it's hard to do well in school," she says. "And if you're worried that you may not live to be eighteen, then what does school matter?"[45]

> "We have a number of students that are struggling with issues associated with traumatic loss or traumatic experiences associated with community violence."[44]
>
> —Courtney Pender, a psychiatric social worker at Washington Prep High School in South Los Angeles, California

PTSD from Bullying

In recent years, much attention has been devoted to the psychological harm to young people who are bullied. Studies have shown that children who are bullied, including cyberbullying, have a higher prevalence of mental health disorders such as depression, anxiety, and PTSD. The youth are also more likely to engage in self-harm and have suicidal thoughts later in life. Dieter Wolke, a British psychologist whose specialty is adolescent bullying, says that even though all young people face conflict and must learn how to resolve it, bullying is different. Its repetitive nature is what makes it so painful and damaging for those who are subjected to it. "Bullying is comparable to a scenario for a caged animal," says Wolke. "The classroom is a place where you're with people you didn't choose to be with, and you can't escape them if something negative happens."[46]

In February 2016 researchers from Hasbro Children's Hospital in Providence, Rhode Island, released a study showing a clear link between cyberbullying and PTSD in teens. The researchers studied

353 adolescents who had been seen in the hospital emergency room (ER). Regardless of why they went to the ER, more than 46 percent reported being physically bullied, 46.7 percent were cyberbullied, and 59 percent were exposed to violence in their communities. An eye-opening finding was that nearly one-fourth of the teens in the ER reported symptoms consistent with PTSD. "This study . . . highlights that teens with a history of cyberbullying or peer violence are more likely to have PTSD,"[47] says Hasbro ER physician Megan Ranney, who led the study.

Bonny O'Donnell, a teenager from Savannah, Georgia, developed PTSD after being relentlessly bullied by her classmates. At the root of their bullying is the girl's personal appearance. She suffers from a hormonal imbalance that causes her to be overweight, and because of that, she has been the target of extreme cruelty. Throughout middle school O'Donnell could hear the bullies' vicious remarks, such as, "Whales are not allowed in shark country."[48] They also told her that no one would miss her if she killed herself—and they dared her to do it.

O'Donnell was tortured by the bullying and plagued repeatedly by nightmares about it, which kept her from sleeping. Sometimes, because she was so tired from lack of sleep, she dozed off at her desk in class. The bullies seized on this opportunity and took pictures of her asleep at her desk, which they posted on social media sites. When she entered high school, the bullying continued. During her freshman year she was hospitalized three times for anxiety and depression, as well as suicidal thoughts. By the time she was diagnosed with PTSD, O'Donnell had become afraid to leave her house.

More Questions than Answers

For decades researchers have studied PTSD and attempted to determine why some young people develop it after enduring trauma when most do not. This research has led to the identification of many factors that contribute to PTSD, including genetics, brain changes, sexual abuse, bullying, and serious accidents, among others. Although scientists still cannot say precisely what causes PTSD, with each new study, the answers become a little clearer.

CHAPTER THREE

What Is It Like to Live with PTSD?

Terrance Thompson, a teenager from Los Angeles, California, has experienced more heartbreak and loss than most people could ever imagine. By the time Thompson was seventeen, the three people he was closest to in the world had died: his mother, his grandmother, and his aunt. While he was growing up, Thompson lived with his mom, who he says was both a mom and dad to him since his dad was hardly ever around. Then his mom died, and he moved in with his grandma and lived with her until she also died. After living with his aunt for a while, she died too, and Thompson narrowly avoided being placed in foster care by moving in with her daughter.

Life has been hard for Thompson, and all the trauma he has endured at such a young age has affected him deeply. As a result, he has been diagnosed with both PTSD and depression. He is quiet, keeps to himself, and often feels like an outcast among his classmates and peers. "People ask me why they can't see my injury when I return from the health center," he says. He finds it uncomfortable to explain about his illness, so most of the time he just avoids socializing with others. He assumes that because he is a loner, people at his school think he is strange, which bothers him. "A lot of people don't know my story," he says, "and it's sad that they kinda talk behind my back, calling me weird and stuff, saying that something is wrong with me." Losing so many people he loved, and then having to cope with the effects of PTSD and depression, has been extremely challenging—and limiting. Thompson says: "It keeps me from doing the stuff I want to do in my life."[49]

A Brutally Honest Description

Like Thompson and other PTSD sufferers, Erika Soderstrom has been negatively affected by PTSD. In fact, the young woman does not hesitate to speak bluntly when describing the effects of the illness: "So, what is it like living with PTSD? Well let's just start with saying that I wouldn't wish it on my worst enemy." Soderstrom describes living with PTSD by using a metaphor. "It's like watching a movie," she says. "You go about your normal day and then all of a sudden you are transported to the worst moment or moments of your life. You sit there and watch this movie that you can't seem to control. Sometimes the entire world seems as if it simply stopped for you to relive these moments." Not all days are exactly the same for Soderstrom, and not all days are necessarily bad. She explains:

> "[PTSD] keeps me from doing the stuff I want to do in my life."[49]
>
> —Terrance Thompson, a teenager from Los Angeles, California, who suffers from PTSD

Certain days I'll have a flashback, recognize it and move on. Other times it's hard to get out of bed. On some occasions the memories just won't stop, like an endless movie playing in my head. On days like that I try to make myself move, get out of bed and face the world. Those days are the hardest days of my life. . . . It hurts, that's all I can say, it just really hurts. It's a specific kind of hell, living with PTSD.[50]

Despite how difficult her life is because of PTSD, Soderstrom tries hard not to dwell on the negative. She says:

On the days that are smooth sailing I remind myself of all the wonderful people I have in my life and all the blessings I have. So when the bad days come I have something to remind me just how [grateful] I should be for the life I have. I could have it much worse and I have had so many privileges in my life. Having said that living with PTSD is nothing easy and it's not a gift in disguise. I have so much ahead of me compared to my past but that trauma will always be a part of me.[51]

Haley's Story

Another young woman who has PTSD is Haley Nystrom. "Living with PTSD is a nightmare of its own," she says. Nystrom was raped as a teen and says that during her first year of college, she was plagued by vivid nightmares of the attack. "I would wake up screaming and thrashing until my roommates rushed to comfort me," she says. Nystrom also suffered from flashbacks so terrifying that she lost consciousness. "I would pass out from shock after flashbacks that were so clear, I could practically reach out and touch my rapist's seemingly tangible face,"[52] she says.

Like many PTSD sufferers, Nystrom also developed chronic anxiety, including panic disorder. She explains, "Though the specific horrors that followed my time undergoing the traumas were still with me, and will probably pop up from time to time throughout the rest of my life, that constant worry became an even larger problem that consumed me." Nystrom's continuous fear, as unfounded as it was, became overpowering. She says:

> My irrational fear that he was coming to kill me kept me up every night. I couldn't comfortably engage in social interactions with men. . . . My relationships suffered and I became a liability. I couldn't go to parties anymore because anything that quickened my heart rate sent me into a panic. I struggled to stay in classrooms, places of employment, and anywhere else that gave me even remote anxiety for longer than 20 minutes before it overcame me.[53]

Holding On to Hope

Young people's lives are affected by trauma in numerous ways, from enduring severe loss to witnessing violent crime or being physically or sexually abused. Some teens develop PTSD after suffering from multiple traumas throughout their lives. This was the case with Ruska (not her real name), a young woman whose childhood and adolescence were filled with emotional, physical, and sexual abuse. "I've had PTSD symptoms as far back as I

The Aftermath of Trauma

The teenage years can be challenging enough for young people. But for those who have lived through a traumatic experience and develop PTSD as a result, life can seem unbearable. Shown here are some of the most common problems associated with trauma-related illnesses like PTSD.

Fear and anxiety	Thinking about the trauma can make teens anxious, and sometimes this anxiety seems to come out of nowhere.
Reexperiencing the traumatic experience	Unwanted thoughts, nightmares, and flashbacks can spring up and serve as vivid reminders of what happened.
Increased arousal	Teens may feel hyper-alert, jumpy, jittery, or shaky, and have trouble concentrating. If this feeling persists, they may get more irritable and have trouble sleeping.
Avoidance	Teens may want to avoid the place where something bad happened, just feel numb, or even avoid all feelings.
Uncontrollable feelings of anger, shame, and/or guilt	Teens may unfairly blame themselves for the traumatic incident and get irritable with people trying to help.
Grief and depression	Teens may feel hopeless, cry often, and lose interest in things and people, even wondering why they should go on. This is a red flag, a sign that they need immediate counseling.
Relationship trouble	Trusting people, feeling good about themselves, and having close relationships may be tough following a traumatic experience. This is normal, and teens must learn to be kind to themselves and not try to mask their feelings with drugs or alcohol.

Source: Sutter Health and Palo Alto Medical Foundation, "Common Problems Following Trauma," October 2015. www.pamf.org.

can remember," she says. Ruska was raped several times while in college, and that was when she was diagnosed with PTSD. When asked how it affects her everyday life, she candidly replies: "It's really hard."[54]

Because of how badly PTSD symptoms were affecting her, Ruska had to take a medical leave from school. She was having severe memory problems and also experiencing blackouts, which are usually associated with alcohol abuse. In her case, however, these were "sober blackouts." Ruska would go about her daily life and have no recollection later of what she had done or said. In addition, she suffered from what is known as dissociation, a

Feeling Alone and Sad

One fourteen-year-old girl who posted anonymously to the online forum Experience Project, where people share their personal experiences, discussed her battle with PTSD. When she was twelve, the girl had surgery to correct a spinal curve, and the operation left her with nerve damage and a partially collapsed lung. The trauma she went through led her to develop nightmares and flashbacks, among other symptoms of PTSD. The girl explained:

> I dont have many friends because my problems are so colossal compared to theirs. I went to see a therapist once but it was so hard for me to talk about it. The weird thing is I remember absolutely everything before and after the surgery. I remember the exact smell, the mood, the taste of the hospital food, I remember everything I said. Its like I am living in the past everyday of my life. I write poetry and I am a very dark person. . . . I cant go back to the hospital! I cant go back to that place! And yes I am only in the 9th grade! I wish i could stop the flashbacks and the bad dreams, i would go back to therapy but I just want to be a kid, I dont want to face my fears! that is about it, I hate my scar, it is 13 inches. I dont want anymore surgery, its like going back to the battlefield.

Believeinme3, "I Am 14 Years Old Living with PTSD," Experience Project, November 29, 2010. www.experience project.com.

defensive state in which someone feels disconnected from his or her own thoughts and actions. She says she had "really bad disassociation. . . . I was completely outside of my body almost looking down on myself."[55] Along with these psychological effects of PTSD, Ruska also suffers from a number of physical ailments, including Crohn's disease (a chronic, painful bowel disease in which the lining of the digestive tract is inflamed); fibromyalgia (chronic muscle pain); celiac disease (an autoimmune disorder in which people cannot tolerate gluten); and chronic fatigue.

Like many young people suffering from PTSD, Ruska developed a severe alcohol problem. This is common among PTSD sufferers; according to the National Center for PTSD, up to 59 percent of young people with the disorder suffer from substance abuse. Often this is because they try to self-medicate, or futilely try to make their troubles disappear by masking them with drugs or alcohol. "When I was drinking," says Ruska, "I was trying to both feel something and numb something at the same time, because I was in so much pain and so numb." She gave up alcohol because whenever she drank, it triggered too many painful memories from the past. "Almost all my abusers were alcoholics," she says. Now in her early twenties, Ruska says that life is getting better, although she still suffers from nightmares and flashbacks. PTSD, she says, "is something very indescribable if you haven't been through it. I feel like there is a lot of judgement about it [and] I'm glad that more word is getting out there about what it's actually like."[56]

Joey's Story

Even among people who are familiar with PTSD, there is low awareness of the variety of experiences that can cause trauma. One example is serious illness; a 2015 study by Johns Hopkins Medicine found that nearly one-quarter of patients who survive a critical illness and a stay in a hospital intensive care unit develop PTSD. "These rates are as high as you might see in combat soldiers or rape victims," says Dale Needham, a Johns Hopkins professor of medicine and physical medicine and rehabilitation. "Our clinicians and patients should know that the high risk of PTSD exists among patients surviving critical illness."[57]

This was the case with Joey, a teenage boy who developed PTSD after surviving a rare type of cancer. When he was ten years old, Joey was diagnosed with Langerhans cell histiocytosis, which caused his white blood cells to attack and destroy his hip bone. Joey underwent bone graft surgery and spent months in a wheelchair afterward, followed by several years of physical therapy. He was assured by his doctors that the disease was gone and would not return, but Joey still fears that it will come back. And since he has met families who lost a child to the same disease, he is afraid that he could die too. Joey, says his mother, "often cries himself to sleep or wakes up with nightmares. The littlest things cause him to worry. He often chooses to hang out by himself in his room

Substance abuse is particularly common among young people suffering with PTSD as a way to self-medicate and mask their troubles.

instead of socializing with others." Joey's mother says he is also plagued by flashbacks, in which he "starts replaying the diagnosis, the surgery, the pain, the time in a wheelchair, therapy and missing out on school and normal things in his mind."[58] Her hope is that in time, Joey will come to accept that he has overcome his illness and will stop spending so much of his time worrying.

Overcoming Despair

Eighteen-year-old Chris is another PTSD sufferer who is plagued by fear, although his is not rooted in illness. Rather, his fear is rooted in memories of an abusive childhood. "Imagine living in a state of constant fear and discomfort," he says, and goes on to describe his life with PTSD:

> You cannot sleep, or perhaps, you sleep too much at times when the nightmares are at bay. Memories plague you, even when you do not wish to think about them. Jumping out at you at improper times, these memories elicit a response of immediate distress. You avoid whatever brings any reminders forth. You cannot interact the same way you used to. You will be on guard, and you may even withdraw from others. Outbursts of anger, sadness, and fear put your loved ones on edge. You have changed, and suddenly, others consider you a burden. Think of these troubles as a snippet of what it is like to live with Post Traumatic Stress Disorder. . . . PTSD interferes with the mental health of the victim in many different ways, and can be quite difficult to cope with.[59]

Until he was in his teens, Chris never realized how abusive his childhood was, nor did he know how profoundly it affected him. "When I thought of trauma," he says, "I thought of deaths, accidents, war, and other horrible experiences I would not have been able to deal with." As the years passed, Chris came to see the truth about his family environment and knew he needed to escape from it. When he was seventeen, he decided to leave home; the environment was "too toxic" for him to handle, so he moved out on his own. "That was, unfortunately, not the end of things," he says, and goes on to explain:

> "PTSD interferes with the mental health of the victim in many different ways, and can be quite difficult to cope with."[59]
>
> —Chris, an eighteen-year-old male with PTSD

> After you leave your abusive situation, the abuse still often sticks to you like cigarette smoke sticks to walls. It lingers there, hollering at you for attention. It only bothered me

43

every once in a while the first few months after I moved out. As time passed, I started to get nightmares every night. I also developed flashbacks, and was reliving previously repressed memories. Having such memories come to surface is very painful and exhausting. I started becoming afraid of everyone around me, flinching at every touch, and crying alone because the pain of what had previously passed was much too great.[60]

When Chris was diagnosed with PTSD, he was stunned and refused to acknowledge that he had the disorder. Eventually, though, he was forced to admit that the therapist was correct. "Instead of continuing with my denial, I accepted what I was being told," he says. "I accepted it, and I cried." Since being diagnosed, he has made progress toward recovery, but he says, "There's not a day that it does not affect me drastically."[61]

Forever Changed

Helaina Hovitz's life was also drastically affected by PTSD after she lived through a terrifying experience. Now in her twenties, Hovitz was a seventh grader in New York City on September 11, 2001, when terrorists flew planes into the World Trade Center. Her school was only three blocks away. Like so many others, she was traumatized by that horrific day. "9/11 seeped into every aspect of my life," she says. "I had moments of deep despair and thoughts of suicide, but there was always a part of me that wouldn't give up hope. The thought that there was a way, somehow, to make a new beginning—that's what kept me going."[62]

> "I had moments of deep despair and thoughts of suicide, but there was always a part of me that wouldn't give up hope."[62]
>
> —Helaina Hovitz, a young woman from New York City who developed PTSD after the 9/11 terrorist attacks

The horrors that Hovitz saw that day, at just twelve years old, are difficult for most people to imagine. With the Twin Towers burning, she and other students were herded outside the school, yet she still did not know what had happened. She saw people jumping to their deaths from the top floors of the skyscrapers and heard deafening booms that shook the ground. Soon the air filled with a giant cloud of smoke and debris, and a friend's

Smoke rises from the fires in the World Trade Center towers during the 9/11 terrorist attack. Many children who witnessed the traumatic events firsthand later exhibited symptoms of PTSD.

mother told Hovitz not to look back but just cover her face and run as fast as she could. Hovitz says:

> The scene for the next hour, as we tried every possible way into our own neighborhood, was the stuff that night-mares are made of: bleeding bodies. People covered in debris, piercing, blood-curdling screams and cries. I was covered in debris and kept forgetting to pull my shirt over my face to protect it. . . . Once we finally made it back to our apartment, we found our neighborhood had become a war zone.[63]

For Hovitz, life after the terrorist attacks was filled with fear, confusion, uncertainty, and anxiety. "The sound of a plane sent me into a hysterical panic," she says, adding that every time she heard a plane, she would hit the floor and start sobbing. "I wasn't sleeping, I was always worried, paranoid, ready to take off at the next attack, having nightmares and flashbacks, feeling like a sitting duck waiting to die." For months, she was afraid to be alone and slept on the floor next to her parents' bed. At the time, it seemed to Hovitz that the rest of New York City and even the world had returned to normal, but that was certainly not the case with her. She explains, "It became very clear to me that because of what was happening in my brain and my body, and what continued to happen outside of my front door, nothing would ever be normal again."[64]

Years passed before Hovitz was diagnosed with PTSD, even though her symptoms were clearly indicative of the disorder. She told therapists about the nightmares that caused her to wake up screaming. She explained about the flashbacks from that horrific day. "I'm nervous all the time," she said during one appointment, "and when I get upset, I feel like I'm out of control. I'm scared of things other people my age aren't scared of. I feel like I'm suffocating half the time. I'm having headaches so often that I've stopped identifying them as headaches."[65] Hovitz was beyond frustrated at the way she was living, and no one could tell her what was wrong. Finally she was diagnosed and was able to begin healing.

Trying to Cope with the Hurt

Teens who live with PTSD are often plagued by negative feelings such as fear, worry, depression, anger, guilt, and shame. They also typically live with side effects such as flashbacks, nightmares, and terrible memories of the traumatic incident. In order to cope, teens may resort to destructive practices such as self-harm, in which they intentionally cut, burn, hit, pierce themselves with needles or pins, or harm themselves in other ways. According to the National Center for PTSD, up to 35 percent of young people engage in self-harm, and rates are higher among those with PTSD. Most often, young people with PTSD who self-harm have a history of childhood neglect or abuse, especially sexual abuse.

The top two reasons most often given by PTSD patients for why they self-harm are to distract themselves from painful feelings and to punish themselves. Research has shown other reasons for self-harming behavior among PTSD sufferers, including efforts to do the following:

- Decrease feelings of numbness or dissociation (feeling like they are outside their body or themselves)
- Reduce stress or tension
- Block upsetting memories and flashbacks
- Show a need for help
- Ensure they will be safe and protected
- Express and release distress
- Reduce anger
- Hurt themselves instead of others

Today the trauma from the terrorist attacks of September 11, 2001, is still with Hovitz, but it is not all-encompassing like it once was. When she walks through a tunnel on the subway or rides an elevator to the top of a high-rise building, she can breathe calmly rather than being too terrified to breathe at all. "The day of 9/11 is something you can never forget—it's too big," she says. "But I have slowly learned to create a life that is better than the one I had when this horrible day happened."[66]

Trying to Move On

Most people do not really understand PTSD because most people, even those who have gone through trauma, do not develop it. Those who have the disorder, however, understand very well that there are hurdles in their lives that sometimes seem too high to climb. This may be a teen who has endured far too many personal losses for his or her young years, lives amidst violent crime, or has suffered from multiple kinds of abuse. Or a young person's trauma may be the residual effect of a life-threatening illness or a devastating terrorist attack in which thousands of people are killed. No matter the cause, teens who have been traumatized often find day-to-day living filled with struggles and challenges. Most learn the importance of never giving up. "I feel very lucky that I never gave up," says Hovitz. "I remember where I came from and I'm proud of myself now. Even after the most awful day we've ever seen, there is life and hope out there."[67]

CHAPTER FOUR

Can PTSD Be Treated or Cured?

Young people who suffer from PTSD could likely be helped if they were treated, but many, perhaps even most, never receive treatment. There are numerous reasons for this, one of which is fear; the decision to open up to someone about PTSD symptoms can be intimidating as well as frightening, and that often prevents teens from seeking help. "It is not uncommon for people with mental health conditions like PTSD to want to avoid talking about it," says the National Center for PTSD. "But getting help for your symptoms is the best thing you can do." The organization goes on to explain that because there are many treatment methods that can help with PTSD, there is no need for the disorder to interfere with people's enjoyment of life, harm their relationships, or cause problems at school or work. "'Getting better' means different things for different people, but people who get treatment improve their quality of life. In many cases, PTSD treatment can get rid of your symptoms."[68]

> "'Getting better' means different things for different people, but people who get treatment improve their quality of life."[68]
>
> —National Center for PTSD, the United States' leading agency for trauma and PTSD research

Working Through the Trauma

Psychotherapy (or just therapy, as it is commonly known) is the standard treatment for most mental illnesses, including PTSD. Therapists may use a number of different types of therapy, depending on the patient's unique needs. "Some people respond better to one type of therapy than another," says the National Alliance on Mental Illness (NAMI), "so a psychotherapist will take things like the nature of the problem being treated and the person's personality into account when determining which treatment will be most effective."[69]

Ruska says that talking to a therapist about her trauma from years of abuse was invaluable in helping her heal. Even though she remembers those events well and continues to have flashbacks, a part of her does not want to believe that the abuse happened. "Talking about it and talking about my feelings helps me to believe it's happened," she says, "accept that it's happened, and therefore let it go. That, mixed with exercising, has been huge for me in allowing me to let off some of that emotion and energy that feels trapped."[70]

Cognitive Behavioral Therapy

One type of therapy that has proved to be especially successful for people with PTSD, including teens, is known as cognitive behavioral therapy (CBT). This technique focuses on helping patients face their fears head-on and teaching them to challenge irrational thoughts and false beliefs in order to permanently change dysfunctional thinking patterns. "By addressing these patterns," says the NAMI, "the person and therapist can work together to develop constructive ways of thinking that will produce healthier behaviors and beliefs. For instance, CBT can help someone replace thoughts that lead to low self-esteem ('I can't do anything right') with positive expectations ('I can do this most of the time, based on my prior experiences')."[71]

Cognitive restructuring therapy is a type of CBT that helps PTSD sufferers make sense of bad memories. "Sometimes people remember the event differently than how it happened," says the National Institute of Mental Health (NIMH). "They may feel guilt or shame about something that is not their fault. The therapist helps people with PTSD cope with their feelings."[72]

Another CBT method, known as eye movement desensitization and reprocessing therapy (EMDR), is often used to treat

PTSD. A number of studies have shown that EMDR can reduce the emotional distress that results from traumatic memories. "EMDR replaces negative emotional reactions to difficult memories with less-charged or positive reactions or beliefs,"[73] says the NAMI. Patients perform a series of back-and-forth, repetitive eye movements for twenty to thirty seconds at a time, which can help them change their emotional reactions.

When Kyler Erickson was being treated for PTSD, he spent three months in EMDR therapy. Twice a week he went into a room with the therapist for an hour, and a light board flashed in different patterns in front of him as he forced himself to relive the school shooting that had so traumatized him in 2011. Journalist

Therapy, particularly CBT, has been proven effective in treating PTSD. This technique helps patients face their fears head-on in order to alter dysfunctional thinking patterns.

Eric Olson writes: "Erickson explained that the treatment caused the memories to gradually shift from the right side of his brain, which is attached to one's emotions, to the left side. Eventually, Erickson could look back at the shooting from a position of strength, as an event he overcame."[74]

Facing Down the Demons

A CBT type known as prolonged exposure therapy helps patients face and control their fears by exposing them to the trauma they experienced in a safe way. They gradually approach the trauma-related feelings, memories, and situations that they have been avoiding since their traumatic experience occurred. This is based

Art and Music Therapy

Art therapy uses drawing, painting, coloring, music, and writing to help people explore their feelings in unique ways. There is no special skill or talent needed, since the artwork that is created is more about the emotions that were felt and expressed during the process. Art therapy is especially helpful for children and teens suffering from PTSD. It is a nonthreatening form of therapy that allows them to examine their own identity, values, morals, and plans for the future. The artwork they create also serves as a way for them to communicate things about themselves or their experiences that may feel too threatening or embarrassing to say out loud.

Jesaca Lepper, a marriage and family therapist, has found music therapy in particular to be effective in treating teens who suffer from PTSD. According to Lepper:

> Music is a very important part of many adolescent lives. It distinguishes what social groups go together and helps many maturing teens express what they feel. In therapy, music can provide a way for therapists to establish a strong relationship with their clients. Music helps adolescents work collectively or express different emotions and aspects of themselves that [they] might have difficulty expressing using traditional talk therapy methods.

Jesaca Lepper, "Why Do Creative Therapies for Teens Work?," Destinations to Recovery, August 17, 2016. www.destinationstorecovery.com.

on the certainty that people with PTSD typically avoid things that remind them of their trauma, which can hamper their recovery from the disorder. By repeatedly discussing their traumatic experience in therapy—including details of what happened and what they thought and felt during the event—and by exposing themselves to activities or situations they have been avoiding because of painful memories, individuals can actually decrease their symptoms of PTSD. According to the NIMH, the technique uses "imagining, writing, or visiting the place where the event happened. The therapist uses these tools to help people with PTSD cope with their feelings."[75]

Exposure therapy can be extraordinarily intimidating for patients at first because, in a sense, they are living the event that traumatized them all over again. It has been shown to be very effective, however, and helps PTSD sufferers learn to deal with memories, thoughts, feelings, and situations related to the traumatic event. Richard J. McNally, a psychological scientist at Harvard University, says that exposure therapy has the "strongest evidence of efficacy"[76] in treating patients with PTSD.

Prolonged exposure therapy consists of weekly individual sessions that usually continue for about three months. It has been shown to help traumatized combat veterans deal with nightmares and flashbacks. Because of its success in helping vets deal with trauma, many therapists are beginning to use prolonged exposure therapy to help teen rape victims who suffer from PTSD. "It almost sounds sadistic—making rape victims as young as 13 relive their harrowing assault over and over," says Lindsey Tanner, a journalist who writes for the *Washington Post*. "But a new study shows it works surprisingly well at eliminating their psychological distress."[77]

This study to which Tanner refers was led by Edna Foa, a University of Pennsylvania psychologist and ardent supporter of exposure therapy in the treatment of PTSD. Foa recruited sixty-one girls aged thirteen to eighteen for the study. All the girls had been raped or sexually abused, and each had been diagnosed with PTSD. The girls were assigned to one of two counseling groups: supportive counseling or prolonged exposure therapy. Each group received fourteen weeks of treatment. Afterward, 83 percent of the girls who received the exposure therapy no longer met the criteria for a PTSD diagnosis. In fact, they recovered at a much higher rate than the girls who received supportive counseling. Only 54 percent in that group were no longer diagnosed with PTSD after their treatment.

Foa notes that at the beginning of the study, many of the girls became upset when discussing what had happened to them. But by talking about their traumatic experience over and over, she says "they get a new perspective of what happened. They get used to thinking and talking about the memory and realizing that it was in the past, that it's not in the present anymore." Eventually, she says, "the story becomes remote, and they get closure."[78]

The fact that many of the girls in the study were initially upset when talking about their experience points to one potential drawback to this form of therapy. In fact, many therapists are reluctant to use exposure therapy with youths because of concerns that it might make their symptoms of PTSD worse. But in an editorial that accompanied the study, Sean Perrin, a psychologist at Lund University in Sweden and a specialist in PTSD treatment in youths, explained that any distress kids may experience is actually a part of the recovery process and usually lessens within a few sessions. Still, Perrin stressed that it is important that exposure therapy be conducted only by a trained and experienced therapist. "A loved one pushing and cajoling another family member to face their fears can actually be unhelpful," Perrin says. "The bottom line is that if you or your child is suffering from anxiety or PTSD, a therapist gradually leading you through exposure, wherein you slowly and willingly confront your fears, can lead to dramatic improvements in functioning without the need for medication."[79]

> "Some physicians will prescribe medications to help with sleep, and at times, medications that quell depressive symptoms or decrease heightened states of arousal are very useful."[80]
>
> —Adolescent psychiatrist Steven Schlozman

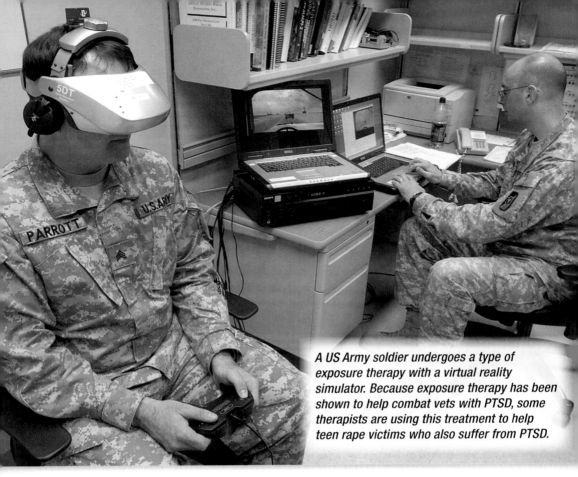

A US Army soldier undergoes a type of exposure therapy with a virtual reality simulator. Because exposure therapy has been shown to help combat vets with PTSD, some therapists are using this treatment to help teen rape victims who also suffer from PTSD.

Psychotherapy and Meds

Yet sometimes medications can be very effective in helping PTSD patients cope with symptoms such as insomnia, anxiety, and depression. "Some physicians will prescribe medications to help with sleep," says adolescent psychiatrist Steven Schlozman, "and at times, medications that quell depressive symptoms or decrease heightened states of arousal are very useful."[80]

Schlozman says that one patient who benefited from a combination of therapy and medications was Sally, the teenage girl from Vermont who suffered from PTSD after the life-threatening car crash with her brother. She underwent weekly psychotherapy sessions with a therapist who specialized in treating traumatized youth. In conjunction with therapy, Sally was prescribed an anti-anxiety medication to help her sleep. After about five weeks her symptoms started to fade, and she was able to return to her nor-

Horses Help Teens Heal

The use of horses in psychotherapy—known as equine therapy—to help treat military veterans with PTSD has gained attention in recent years, and now equine therapy is being used to help children and teens with PTSD too. With equine therapy, the horses are usually not ridden and are not tethered, or tied, in the arena but are allowed to walk free. A simple exercise consists of the PTSD patient approaching a horse and putting a halter on it. Some kids, especially those who have experienced severe trauma, may be afraid of the horses at first, but horses' natural gentleness and affection helps put these fears to rest. And learning to trust an animal through equine therapy can help youths with PTSD develop or regain the trust they may have lost in others due to the trauma of physical or sexual abuse, abandonment, or neglect.

Equine therapy helped one fifteen-year-old girl who suffered from the aftereffects of trauma and had become suicidal. The girl was a patient at Solstice East, a residential treatment center in North Carolina for teen girls struggling with PTSD and other emotional or behavioral problems. Her therapist, Katie Hornowski, describes the success of equine therapy in this instance: "In working with the horses, we were able to break through to underlying issues. Horses have a unique ability to help our students see their patterns and be more open to their emotions. . . . With the horses, we were able to help this student regulate her emotions and have more insight into herself."

Quoted in Solstice East, "Equine Therapy Success Story." http://solsticeeast.com.

mal routine. "The automobile accident would always play a role in her life's story," says Schlozman, "but now she could tolerate that story without the accompanying symptoms and challenges."[81]

Teens and Vets Helping Each Other

Along with traditional treatment methods, such as different types of therapy and medications, alternative treatments have proved to be successful at treating teens with PTSD. One of these is an innovative program called Urban Warriors, which originated in Chicago, Illinois. The sixteen-week program, which is part of the YMCA of Metro Chicago's Youth Safety and Violence Prevention (YSVP) initiative, pairs youth who have been exposed to violence with military veterans who have been in combat. During their weekly meetings, the teens and the veterans discuss and process their experiences with violence, as well as share and develop methods of coping with their trauma. Prior to the sessions the vets, who act as mentors to the teens, receive training and support from YSVP staff members.

The Urban Warriors program was created by Eddie Bocanegra, a former gang member who now serves as coexecutive director of youth safety and violence prevention at the Chicago YMCA. When he was nineteen, Bocanegra was sentenced to prison for felony murder. While serving his sentence, he was frequently visited by his brother, a decorated army veteran who had done two tours of duty in Iraq. In talking to his brother, Bocanegra began to realize that kids exposed to violence on the streets could struggle with PTSD in much the same way as combat veterans. And because these two groups share common life experiences—struggling to cope in a hostile, often violent environment—Bocanegra believed that both the youths and the vets could benefit from being brought together to discuss their experiences.

Bocanegra knew that many Chicago youths live in dangerous neighborhoods where violence is common. In fact, in 2015 Chicago had the highest murder rate of any city in the nation, with 469 murders and 2,900 shootings. In one group of forty-one youths who participated in an Urban Warriors program in 2015, thirty-six said they had either witnessed or heard about the violent death of a loved one. In many teens, an experience such as this can cause symptoms that parallel those of veterans with PTSD.

By early 2016 more than eighty youths had participated in Chicago's Urban Warriors program. The program follows a structured curriculum that consists of five basic themes: belonging, positive identity development, cognitive restructuring, coping, and community engagement. During the weekly sessions, youths participate in various activities that include exploring feelings through artwork; team-building exercises, such as playing tug-of-war; and meeting in group sessions with veteran mentors. "I know for a fact that these kids sit down and lay down their head at night, and they think about what we talk about," says Lance Corporal Richard Rivera, a US Marine Corps veteran who serves as a mentor for the program. It is not only the kids who are helped by the program—the veterans derive benefit from talking about their traumatic experiences, too. And for mentors like Rivera, there is also a sense of personal accomplishment involved. "I feel like I've done something positive, like, besides fighting for my country,"[82] he says.

One of the program's mentors is Mikhail Dasovich, a twenty-five-year-old Marine Corps veteran who has suffered from PTSD. He describes what happened the first time he led a group session for the program: "I was very, very nervous, and all of the youth were looking at me. And everyone's clowning, everyone's joking. And one of the youth . . . he says to me like, 'Hey, you ever seen someone get shot in front of you?' And the whole room went silent, and I was like 'Oh man, like, this quick, huh?" Dasovich answered the question by telling the group a story about being deployed in a war zone—how he had watched his platoon sergeant get shot right in front of him. "I went into detail," says Dasovich, "what seeing my father figure getting tore up by rifle bullets, what that did to me emotionally." The teen who had asked the pointed question then shared a story of his own, as Dasovich explains: "Right from my answer [he] goes in to describe how he had to watch his two cousins get gunned down right in front of him. And that was something I had never felt before, to have such a young man so effortlessly describe the execution of his family members." He adds: "These kids, before they're 16, have, in essence, really been to combat."[83]

One teen who found the Urban Warriors program helpful is fifteen-year-old Jim Courtney-Clarks, who lives in the East Garfield Park neighborhood, a particularly violent area of the city. "Every time you look up somebody else is getting killed, and I never know if it's me or somebody I am really close to," he explains. But Courtney-Clarks says the Urban Warriors program has changed his outlook on the future. "The past week, I was just thinking about dropping out of school," he says. "Until today. And I see that it's a lot of stuff that I can accomplish if I stay in school, by looking at the veterans.

Like I'm not sure if I want to go to college, but I might want to join the police academy or just go to the Navy or something."[84]

Promising Discoveries

There are a number of innovative treatment programs throughout the United States that are helping young PTSD sufferers heal and finally have hope. Another important facet in helping youth with PTSD is research, which is ongoing and has yielded some exciting discoveries about treatment of the disorder. "In the last decade," says the NIMH, "progress in research on the mental and biological foundations of PTSD has led scientists to focus on better understanding the underlying causes of why people experience a range of reactions to trauma."[85] The NIMH adds that researchers are exploring many different aspects of PTSD prevention and treatment.

One focus of PTSD research is the benefits of nature in helping reduce the disorder in combat veterans, as well as in inner-city

Research has shown that spending time in nature has lessened PTSD symptoms in combat veterans, as well as young people who have been exposed to violence.

teens who have been exposed to violence. A study launched in 2014 by Craig Anderson, a psychology doctoral student at the University of California–Berkeley, involves two dozen war veterans and more than ninety inner-city Bay Area middle and high school students. The researchers observed changes in the participants during and after one- or two-day whitewater rafting trips down the North Fork American River near Sacramento, California. The researchers studied footage from cameras attached to participants' helmets during the rafting trips and coded hundreds of hours of video based on facial expressions, body language, and interactions with other people during the trips. Study participants were also surveyed before the trips and asked to rate things such as their well-being, how well they got along with others, how they were sleeping, and their general sense of happiness.

Researchers followed up with the participants one week after the trip via e-mail and asked them the same set of questions in order to gauge the changes participants experienced. Both the vets and the teens reported a decrease in their PTSD symptoms and stress levels, as well as an improvement in their sleep. And veterans and teens alike reported feeling a sense of awe during their rafting trips and later noted that they got along better with their friends and families. "If doctors were able to write prescriptions for people to get out in nature, it would be one of the most cost-effective health interventions available, and would change our relationship to the outdoors,"[86] says Anderson.

> "[Trauma] is an invisible, internal wound. And it takes time, patience and caring to heal."[89]
>
> —Gretchen Schmelzer, a psychologist and trauma expert

In addition, participants in the study showed positive changes in measures of stress hormones, immune function, and dopamine regulators during and after the trips. Specifically, researchers measured levels of the stress hormone cortisol—and actually found that higher levels of cortisol were associated with positive emotions after the rafting trip. "It's an adaptive hormone," Anderson explains. "When we sit in front of computers being stressed out, cortisol doesn't help us. But when we're out in nature and we need more energy to achieve something physically demanding, cortisol goes up in a good way."[87]

Participants experienced emotions ranging from fear to curiosity to joy during the whitewater rafting trips. For many of the inner-city teens, who were used to putting on a tough exterior around their peers in order to protect themselves, the act of opening themselves up to a new and fun experience seemed like a daunting task at first. But the rush of adrenaline and the sense of togetherness the teens experienced while working to navigate the rapids without falling out of the rafts helped them move beyond their troubles. Anderson was pleased when one of the youths, who was initially reluctant to go on the rafting trip, asked him afterward, "How could something scary feel so good?"[88]

Tomorrow Can Be Better

Teens suffering from PTSD may feel hopeless and despondent, thinking that this is the way life will always be. Because of the trauma they have been through, and the ways they have suffered because of it, such a perspective is understandable. Trauma, says psychologist Gretchen Schmelzer, "is an invisible, internal wound. And it takes time, patience and caring to heal."[89]

There was a time when Terrance Thompson was so consumed with grief and loss that he had little hope for a better future. Then, because of a treatment program offered at his high school in South Los Angeles, he began to see that maybe things could get better after all. By participating in both individual and group therapy, he started making progress and began to get his life back on track. Therapy taught him that he is not crazy, strange, or weird, as he had assumed others thought. He learned that he is not alone and that many other young people suffer from PTSD just as he does. Thompson's improvement has been remarkable; his confidence has improved, and so has his attitude and hope for the future. Filmmaker Joris Debeij, who featured Thompson in a documentary called *I Am Los Angeles*, writes: "His story so far has been dominated with the need to cope with past and present, though he looks forward to a day when he can comprehend what he wants for his future."[90] Many other young PTSD sufferers look forward to that day, too.

SOURCE NOTES

Introduction: A Living Nightmare

1. Quoted in Theresa Vargas, "'Don't Kill Her!' Children Who Witness Domestic Violence Carry Lifelong Scars," *Washington Post*, March 8, 2014. www.washingtonpost.com.
2. Gretchen Schmelzer, "When Your Teen Is Living with Trauma," *Gretchen Schmelzer* (blog), September 14, 2015. http://gretchenschmelzer.com.
3. Anxiety and Depression Association of America, "Posttraumatic Stress Disorder (PTSD)," June 2016. www.adaa.org.
4. Edgar Jones, "Shell Shocked," American Psychological Association, June 2012. www.apa.org.
5. Quoted in Eric Jaffe, "Gen. Patton's 1943 Memo Accusing Mental Casualties of Cowardice," *Slate*, January 15, 2014. www.slate.com.
6. Matthew J. Friedman, "PTSD History and Overview," National Center for PTSD, February 23, 2016. www.ptsd.va.gov.
7. Quoted in Eyama Harris, "PTSD Isn't Just a War Wound; Teens Suffer, Too," *All Things Considered*, NPR, August 17, 2012. www.npr.org.

Chapter One: What Is PTSD?

8. Quoted in Eric Olson, "PTSD in Past, Neb-Omaha Player Advocates for Mental Wellness," CNS News, March 1, 2016. www.cnsnews.com.
9. Quoted in Melissa Fry, "Teen Copes with PTSD After Millard South Deadly Shooting," KETV, May 8, 2014. www.ketv.com.
10. Stefanie Bagley, "What Do You Think When You Hear PTSD?," *A Beautiful Rant* (blog), 2015. http://abeautifulrant.tumblr.com.
11. Matthew Tull, "The Fight or Flight Response: Our Body's Response to Stress," Very Well, November 25, 2014. www.verywell.com.

12. Tull, "The Fight or Flight Response."
13. Tull, "The Fight or Flight Response."
14. Cat P., "When PTSD Means You Are in Constant Fight-or-Flight Mode," *Mighty*, August 2016. https://themighty.com.
15. Sara Staggs, "Symptoms & Diagnosis of PTSD," Psych Central, July 17, 2016. http://psychcentral.com.
16. Roy H. Lubit, "Posttraumatic Stress Disorder in Children," Medscape, May 19, 2016. http://emedicine.medscape.com.
17. Stanford Children's Health, "Post-Traumatic Stress Disorder in Children," 2016. www.stanfordchildrens.org.
18. Quoted in Fry, "Teen Copes with PTSD After Millard South Deadly Shooting."
19. Shaili Jain, "What Dreams May Come: Treating the Nightmares of PTSD," *Mind the Brain* (blog), PLOS, November 19, 2013. http://blogs.plos.org.
20. Steven Schlozman, "What Is Post-Traumatic Stress Disorder (PTSD)?," Clay Center for Young Healthy Minds, October 28, 2013. www.mghclaycenter.org.
21. David Riggs, "Post-Traumatic Stress Disorder," Mental Health America, 2016. www.mentalhealthamerica.net.
22. National Center for PTSD, "What Is PTSD?," July 13, 2016. www.ptsd.va.gov.
23. Brain & Behavior Research Foundation, "Frequently Asked Questions About Post-Traumatic Stress Disorder (PTSD)," 2016. https://bbrfoundation.org.
24. Eyama Harris, "PTSD Isn't Just a War Wound; Teens Suffer Too," NPR, August 17, 2012. www.npr.org.
25. Elements Behavioral Health, "Teens, Younger Kids Can Get PTSD, Too," 2016. www.elementsbehavioralhealth.com.
26. Schlozman, "What Is Post-Traumatic Stress Disorder (PTSD)?"
27. Child Trends DataBank, "Children's Exposure to Violence," May 2016. www.childtrends.org.
28. Abdelaziz Thabet, Omar EL-Buhaisi, and Panos Vostanis, "Trauma, PTSD, Anxiety and Coping Strategies Among Palestinian Adolescents Exposed to War in Gaza," *Arab Journal of Psychiatry*, May 2014. www.arabjpsychiat.com/media/PDF/2014_n/the_arab_journal_2014.pdf.

Chapter Two: What Causes PTSD?

29. Daniel Busso, "Who Is Most at Risk for PTSD After Trauma? Lessons from the Boston Marathon Bombings," *Vector* (blog), Boston Children's Hospital, August 20, 2014. http://vector.childrenshospital.org.
30. Matthew J. Friedman, "PTSD History and Overview," National Center for PTSD, February 23, 2016. www.ptsd.va.gov.
31. Schmelzer, "When Your Teen Is Living with Trauma."
32. Schlozman, "What Is Post-Traumatic Stress Disorder (PTSD)?"
33. National Center for PTSD, "PTSD in Children and Teens," August 13, 2015. www.ptsd.va.gov.
34. Julian D. Ford, "Trauma Exposure and Posttraumatic Stress Disorder in the Lives of Adolescents," *Child & Adolescent Psychiatry*, August 2013. www.jaacap.com.
35. Busso, "Who Is Most at Risk for PTSD After Trauma? Lessons from the Boston Marathon Bombings."
36. Busso, "Who Is Most at Risk for PTSD After Trauma? Lessons from the Boston Marathon Bombings."
37. Susanne Babbel, "Trauma: Childhood Sexual Abuse," *Somatic Psychology* (blog), *Psychology Today*, March 12, 2013. www.psychologytoday.com.
38. Delphine Collin-Vézina, Isabelle Daigneault, and Martine Hébert, "Lessons Learned from Child Sexual Abuse Research: Prevalence, Outcomes, and Preventive Strategies," *Child and Adolescent Psychiatry and Mental Health*, July 18, 2013. www.ncbi.nlm.nih.gov.
39. Collin-Vézina et al., "Lessons Learned from Child Sexual Abuse Research."
40. Harold Cohen, "Two Stories of PTSD," Psych Central, July 17, 2016. http://psychcentral.com.
41. Cohen, "Two Stories of PTSD."
42. Quoted in Anxiety BC, "Post-Traumatic Stress Disorder and Young People," 2015. www.heretohelp.bc.ca.
43. Quoted in Stephen Stock, Michael Bott, Mark Villareal, and Jeremy Carroll, "Oakland Gun Violence Victims Suffer Continuous PTSD," NBC Bay Area News, August 4, 2016. www.nbcbayarea.com.

44. Courtney Pender, interview, *I Am Los Angeles*, 2015. www
    .iamlosangeles.com.
45. Pender, interview.
46. Quoted in Ashley Strickland, "Bullying by Peers Has Effects
    Later in Life," CNN, May 8, 2015. www.cnn.com.
47. Quoted in Hasbro Children's Hospital, "Hasbro Children's
    Hospital Study Finds Nearly Half of All Teens Visiting Emer-
    gency Department Report Peer Violence and Cyberbullying,
    Many Showing Signs of PTSD," news release, February 18,
    2016. www.hasbrochildrenshospital.org.
48. Quoted in Sarah Kershaw, "Bullied by Classmates, This Geor-
    gia Teen Can Now Bring Her Service Dog 'Carson' to School
    to Cope," *Washington Post*, January 11, 2016. www.wash
    ingtonpost.com.

Chapter Three: What Is It Like to Live with PTSD?

49. Terrance Thompson, "Terrance," *I Am Los Angeles*, 2015.
    www.iamlosangeles.com.
50. Erika Soderstrom, "What It's like to Live with PTSD as a Young
    Adult," Odyssey Online, February 10, 2016. www.theodyssey
    online.com.
51. Soderstrom, "What It's like to Live with PTSD as a Young
    Adult."
52. Haley Nystrom, "What It's like Living with PTSD," Odyssey
    Online, July 7, 2015. www.theodysseyonline.com.
53. Nystrom, "What It's like Living with PTSD."
54. Quoted in Dana Dovey, "A Day in the Life of a PTSD Patient:
    Flashbacks, Discomfort, and Hope," Medical Daily, August
    27, 2015. www.medicaldaily.com.
55. Quoted in Dovey, "A Day in the Life of a PTSD Patient."
56. Quoted in Dovey, "A Day in the Life of a PTSD Patient."
57. Quoted in Johns Hopkins Medicine, "PTSD Common in ICU
    Survivors," news release, April 20, 2015. www.hopkinsmedi
    cine.org.
58. Gina Stegner, "Coping with PTSD," *Cincinnati Family*, March
    30, 2015. http://cincinnatifamilymagazine.com.

59. Chris, "The Complexity of Human Experience—PTSD," *Mental Health & Coping* (blog), Mind Your Mind, July 27, 2015. https://mindyourmind.ca.

60. Chris, "The Complexity of Human Experience—PTSD."

61. Chris, "The Complexity of Human Experience—PTSD."

62. Quoted in Cathy Free, "Child Survivor of 9/11 Finds Her Way Back After Struggling with PTSD: 'There Is Life and Hope out There,'" *People*, September 6, 2016. www.people.com.

63. Helaina Hovitz, "How Surviving 9/11 as a Kid Messed with My Head," *Vice*, September 9, 2016. www.vice.com.

64. Hovitz, "How Surviving 9/11 as a Kid Messed with My Head."

65. Hovitz, "How Surviving 9/11 as a Kid Messed with My Head."

66. Quoted in Free, "Child Survivor of 9/11 Finds Her Way Back After Struggling with PTSD."

67. Quoted in Free, "Child Survivor of 9/11 Finds Her Way Back After Struggling with PTSD."

Chapter Four: Can PTSD Be Treated or Cured?

68. National Center for PTSD, "What's Stopping You? Overcome Barriers to Care," August 14, 2015. www.ptsd.va.gov.

69. National Alliance on Mental Illness, "Psychotherapy," 2015. www.nami.org.

70. Quoted in Dovey, "A Day in the Life of a PTSD Patient."

71. National Alliance on Mental Illness, "Psychotherapy."

72. National Institute of Mental Health, "Post-Traumatic Stress Disorder," 2016. www.nimh.nih.gov.

73. National Alliance on Mental Illness, "Psychotherapy."

74. Olson, "PTSD in Past, Neb-Omaha Player Advocates for Mental Wellness."

75. National Institute of Mental Health, "Post-Traumatic Stress Disorder."

76. Quoted in Association for Psychological Science, "The Facts About Prolonged Exposure Therapy for PTSD," *Observations*, January 26, 2015. www.psychologicalscience.org.

77. Lindsey Tanner, "Therapy Used to Treat Vets with PTSD Helps Teen Rape Victims, Study Says," *Washington Post*, December 25, 2013. www.washingtonpost.com.

78. Quoted in Tanner, "Therapy Used to Treat Vets with PTSD Helps Teen Rape Victims, Study Says."

79. Quoted in Alan Mozes, "Therapy That Confronts Trauma of Sexual Abuse Helped Teen Girls with PTSD," MedicineNet, December 24, 2013. www.medicinenet.com.

80. Schlozman, "What Is Post-Traumatic Stress Disorder (PTSD)?"

81. Schlozman, "What Is Post-Traumatic Stress Disorder (PTSD)?"

82. Quoted in YMCA of Metro Chicago, "Urban Warriors," 2016. www.ymcachicago.org.

83. Quoted in Audie Cornish, "Chicago Teens and Combat Veterans Join Forces to Process Trauma," *All Things Considered*, NPR, January 25, 2016. www.npr.org.

84. Quoted in Cornish, "Chicago Teens and Combat Veterans Join Forces to Process Trauma."

85. National Institute of Mental Health, "Post-Traumatic Stress Disorder."

86. Quoted in Yasmin Anwar, "Rush of Wild Nature Lowers PTSD in Veterans, At-Risk Teens," Medical Xpress, June 1, 2016. http://medicalxpress.com.

87. Quoted in Anwar, "Rush of Wild Nature Lowers PTSD in Veterans, At-Risk Teens."

88. Quoted in Anwar, "Rush of Wild Nature Lowers PTSD in Veterans, At-Risk Teens."

89. Schmelzer, "When Your Teen Is Living with Trauma."

90. Joris Debeij, "I Didn't Even Know What I Was Going Through," *Atlantic*, October 27, 2014. www.theatlantic.com.

RECOGNIZING SIGNS OF TROUBLE

- Frightening thoughts or memories
- Vivid flashbacks of the traumatic event
- Feelings of hopelessness
- Irritability; being easily startled
- Appearing jittery or hyperactive
- Avoiding situations that remind him or her of the traumatic event
- Avoiding activities that previously were enjoyable
- Problems staying asleep and nightmares
- Trouble concentrating
- Problems in school, declining grades
- Relationship problems, including those with family and friends
- Anxiety and/or panic
- Aggression and hostility
- Sadness, depression, or irrational fear
- Physical ailments, such as stomachaches, headaches, or chronic pain
- Problems with drinking and/or drugs
- Running away from home

ORGANIZATIONS TO CONTACT

The following organizations offer help for teens and others suffering from PTSD, as well as detailed information about this disorder.

American Psychological Association (APA)
750 First St. NE
Washington, DC 20002
website: www.apa.org

The APA is the largest scientific and professional organization that represents the field of psychology in the United States. Its website links to newspaper articles, research data, and a number of online publications that focus on PTSD.

Centers for Disease Control and Prevention (CDC)
1600 Clifton Rd.
Atlanta, GA 30333
website: www.cdc.gov

The CDC is a federal agency charged with protecting the health of Americans. Its website contains a section titled "Children's Mental Health" that includes basic information on PTSD symptoms, treatment, and prevention.

Mayo Clinic
200 First St. SW
Rochester, MN 55905
website: www.mayoclinic.org

The Mayo Clinic is the world's largest nonprofit medical group practice. Its website includes a section titled "Post-Traumatic Stress Disorder," which contains information on causes, risk factors, and treatment; tips on coping and support; a blog; and numerous links to other websites and organizations that help individuals cope with PTSD.

Mental Health America

2000 N. Beauregard St., 6th Floor
Alexandria, VA 22311
website: www.mentalhealthamerica.net

Formed in 1909, Mental Health America is the nation's oldest advocacy organization that addresses mental health. Its website contains numerous resources related to PTSD, including basic facts, tips on how to get help, and links to numerous other organizations that deal with traumatic stress.

Minding Your Mind (MYM)

42 W. Lancaster Ave., 2nd Floor
Ardmore, PA 19003
website: http://mindingyourmind.org

MYM provides mental health education to children, teens, young adults, and their parents; teachers; and school administrators. The organization offers educational programs that cover numerous issues, including PTSD. Its website provides several resources, including news, events, a blog, and a section on mental health basics for students.

MyPTSD

website: www.myptsd.com

MyPTSD is an online community where teens (and adults) can seek peer support from others suffering from PTSD. The website offers various forums, as well as information on the causes, symptoms, treatments, and risk factors associated with PTSD.

National Alliance on Mental Illness (NAMI)

3803 N. Fairfax Dr., Suite 100
Arlington, VA 22203
website: www.nami.org

The NAMI is a nonprofit advocacy group for families and people affected by mental illness in the United States. The NAMI website includes its Child & Adolescent Action Center (CAAC), which works to improve the lives of children, teens, and young adults impacted by mental illness. The CAAC offers an Internet resource list that includes links to numerous federal agencies and organizations concerned with children's and teens' mental health.

National Center for PTSD

US Department of Veterans Affairs
810 Vermont Ave. NW
Washington, DC 20420
website: www.ptsd.va.gov

The National Center for PTSD is the United States' leading agency for trauma and PTSD research. A wealth of information about PTSD, including PTSD in teens, can be found on its website, such as a search engine that produces numerous articles about PTSD.

National Child Traumatic Stress Network (NCTSN)

NCCTS—Duke University
411 W. Chapel Hill St., Suite 200
Durham, NC 27701
website: www.nctsn.org

The NCTSN works to improve access to care, treatment, and services for children and teens exposed to traumatic events. Its website contains a multitude of resources, including information on the various types of traumatic stress, an e-bulletin, news, upcoming events, research, articles about children and traumatic stress, and numerous links for more information.

National Institute of Mental Health (NIMH)

6001 Executive Blvd., Room 6200, MSC 9663
Bethesda, MD 20892
website: www.nimh.nih.gov

An agency of the US Department of Health and Human Services, the NIMH is the largest research organization in the world specializing in mental illness. The NIMH website's "Child and Adolescent Mental Health" section contains news, studies, several publications for children and teens, information on types of treatment, and several links for more information on PTSD.

FOR FURTHER RESEARCH

Books

Joan Esherick, *Managing Stress*. Broomall, PA: Mason Crest, 2014.

Helaina Hovitz, *After 9/11: One Girl's Journey Through Darkness to a New Beginning*. New York: Carell.

H.W. Poole, *Post-Traumatic Stress Disorder*. Broomall, PA: Mason Crest, 2016.

Bessel van der Kolk, *The Body Keeps the Score: Brain, Mind, and Body in the Healing of Trauma*. New York: Penguin, 2016.

David Walker, *PTSD*. Seattle, WA: Amazon, 2016. Kindle edition.

Mary Beth Williams and Soili Poijula, *The PTSD Workbook: Simple, Effective Techniques for Overcoming Traumatic Stress Symptoms*. Oakland, CA: New Harbinger, 2016.

Internet Sources

Sue Ambrose, "Tornadoes' Aftermath Puts Some at Risk for PTSD," *Dallas (TX) Morning News*, January 25, 2016. www.dallasnews.com/lifestyles/health-and-fitness/health/20160125-tornadoes-aftermath-puts-some-at-risk-for-ptsd.ece.

Daniella David and Spencer Eth, "PTSD Not Just for Soldiers, Can Affect Anyone," *Miami (FL) Herald*, June 20, 2016. www.miamiherald.com/living/health-fitness/article84935957.html.

Cathy Free, "Child Survivor of 9/11 Finds Her Way Back After Struggling with PTSD: 'There Is Life and Hope Out There,'" *People*, September 6, 2016. www.people.com/article/helaina-hovitz-911-ptsd-recovery.

Jessica Hamblen, "PTSD in Children and Teens," National Center for PTSD, 2015. www.ptsd.va.gov/public/family/ptsd-children-adolescents.asp.

Alice Park, "How Fireworks Can Trigger PTSD," *Time*, July 2, 2015. time.com/3945001/fireworks-ptsd.

Rick Pollard, "Violent Newstream Could Cause Symptoms of PTSD in Teens," Solstice East, July 19, 2016. http://solsticeeast .com/violent-newstream-causing-symptoms-ptsd-in-teens.

Robert Preidt, "Mindfulness Training May Ease PTSD," *U.S. News & World Report*, April 1, 2016. http://health.usnews.com/health -news/articles/2016-04-01/mindfulness-training-may-ease-ptsd.

Christina Procopiou, "Earthquake Survivors with PTSD Have Altered Brains," *Newsweek*, March 2, 2016. www.newsweek.com /brains-changed-earthquake-survivors-ptsd-432653.

Donovan X. Ramsey, "Recovering from PTSD After Hurricane Katrina," *Atlantic*, September 1, 2015. www.theatlantic.com/health /archive/2015/09/ptsd-after-hurricane-katrina/403162.

Right Step, "Teens Involved in Vehicle Crashes at Higher Risk for Developing Mental Disorders," June 11, 2015. www.rightstep .com/teen-mental-health/teens-involved-in-vehicle-crashes-at -higher-risk-for-developing-mental-disorders.

Shira Schoenberg, "2 Years Later, 'Invisible' Wounds Plague Boston Marathon Bombing Victims," MassLive.com, June 25, 2015. www.masslive.com/news/boston/index.ssf/2015/06/two_years _later_invisible_woun.html.

Melody Schreiber, "She Found Relief for PTSD with a Different Kind of Therapy. But Does It Work?," *Washington Post*, August 1, 2016. www.washingtonpost.com/national/health -science/she-found-relief-for-ptsd-with-a-different-kind-of-ther apy-but-does-it-work/2016/08/01/97e7df60-1aca-11e6-8c7b -6931e66333e7_story.html.

Jeanette Steele, "PTSD: What's Working, What's Ahead?," *San Diego (CA) Union-Tribune*, June 13, 2016. www.sandiegounion tribune.com/news/2016/jun/13/ptsd-therapy-veterans-affairs -treatment.

Tampa Bay (FL) Times, "Service Dog Eases Teen's PTSD from Bullying," January 25, 2016. www.beaches.tampabay.com/features /pets/service-dog-eases-teens-ptsd-from-bullying/2262704.

Teen Rehab Center, "PTSD in Teens: Types, Symptoms & Treatment Options," 2016. www.teenrehabcenter.org/co-occurring -disorders/ptsd.

Robert F. Worth, "What If PTSD Is More Physical than Psychological?,'" *New York Times Magazine*, June 10, 2016. www.nytimes .com/2016/06/12/magazine/what-if-ptsd-is-more-physical-than -psychological.html.

INDEX

PICTURE CREDITS

Cover: Depositphotos/michaeldb

 6: Shutterstock.com/Gina Jacobs

11: iStockphoto/monkeybusinessimages

15: Maury Aaseng

20: Aleppo Media Center/Associated Press

25: Maury Aaseng

29: Thinkstock Images/iStock

34: Thinkstock Images/iStock

39: Maury Aaseng

42: Thinkstock Images/Monkey Business

45: Shutterstock.com/Dan Howell

51: Thinkstock Images/Monkey Business

55: US Army/Science Photo Library

59: Thinkstock Images/iStock

Peggy J. Parks holds a bachelor of science degree from Aqui-nas College in Grand Rapids, Michigan, where she graduated magna cum laude. An author who has written dozens of educa-tional books on a wide variety of topics for young people, Parks lives in Muskegon, Michigan, a town she says inspires her writing because of its location on the shores of beautiful Lake Michigan.

MB
mar/18